Military Aircraft
In Detail
Variants • Weapons • Equipment

Henschel
Hs 129

'The Henschel Hs 129? It was an airborne jewel! I cannot compare it to any of the dozen other aircraft types I flew while I was a combat pilot.

'How did it fly? Well, I firmly believe everyone who flew it – not only me – remained equally enchanted and in love with it the same way I was. As a fighting tool, it was unparalleled in its category. (...)

'The Hs 129 B-2 had extraordinary manoeuvrability, it was fully suited for aerobatics, visibility was perfect, firepower was great, even compared to aircraft in the same category we had encountered, like the Soviet Il-2 Shturmovik. (...)

'The results achieved by us with the Henschel were praised initially by the German High Command, then [after Rumania's defection from the Axis camp on 23 August 1944], ironically, by the Soviets, as well.'

(*Adjutant aviator* Vasile Anghel, veteran of the Rumanian *Grupul 8 asalt*, and Henschel Hs 129 pilot for over two years, in a letter dated 1978).

Military Aircraft

In Detail

Variants • Weapons • Equipment

Henschel Hs 129

Dénes Bernád

Acknowledgements   The author would like to acknowledge the invaluable assistance of the
following individuals who helped with information or photographs (in
alphabetical order): Mihai Andrei, Vasile Anghel [deceased], Miroslav Bíly,
Razvan Bujor, Lutz Budraß, Sven Carlsen, Carl Charles, Eddie Creek, Hans-
Peter Dabrowski, Carl-Fredrik Geust, Dmitry Grinyuk, Bjørn Hafsten,
Rainer Haufschild, Tony Jones, Kees Mol, Lazar Munteanu [deceased],
Günther Ott, Martin Pegg, James Perry, Peter Petrick, György Punka,
Jean-Louis Roba, Matti Salonen, Gerhard Stemmer, Ion Taralunga
[deceased], Ferenc-Antal Vajda, Tom Willis and László Winkler [deceased].

First published 2006

ISBN 1 85780 238 1
ISBN 978 1 85780 238 2

Produced by Chevron Publishing Limited

Project Editors: Eddie J. Creek and Mark Nelson/Chevron Publishing

© Narrative text: Dénes Bernád
© Line artwork: Arthur Bentley
  Enthusiasts can order the line drawings found in this publication and
  Arthur Bentley's other extensive aviation line art by going to
  www.albentley-drawings.com
© Colour Profiles: Tom Tullis

Published by Midland Publishing
an imprint of Ian Allan Publishing Ltd. Hersham, Surrey, KT12 4RG

Printed in England by Ian Allan Printing Ltd, Hersham, Surrey KT12 4RG

Visit the Ian Allan Publishing at www.ianallanpublishing.com

MIDLAND
An imprint of
Ian Allan Publishing
www.ianallanpublishing.com

Contents

Genesis of a Tank-Killer

"... in the early stage, it appears that the Focke-Wulf hybrid project was preferred over Henschel's original design. This was mainly due to the possibility of producing the reconnaissance version of the Fw 189 in parallel with the assault version, the powerplants and main structural parts – except for the cockpit – being identical."

▽ Individual nicknames assigned to the Hs 129 were rare but this pilot has painted the word 'Mülle' (rubbish) on the side of his aircraft's yellow nose.

The Spanish Civil War of 1936-1939 was politically the opening stage of an overall world conflagration. From a military point of view, the conflict was a unique chance for the involved parties to experiment with the latest war doctrines, particularly the large-scale use of air power. Spain was also an ideal testing ground for a large variety of innovative warfare technologies, including combat aircraft. It was also in Spain that the need for close air-support for one's own advancing or retreating combat troops had first emerged.

The task of destroying fixed or slowly moving smaller targets such as ships, for example, was solved by employing the dive-bombing technique with its pinpoint accuracy, carried out by the *Sturzkampfflugzeug*, or *Stuka* – as the famous, or infamous, Junkers Ju 87 is widely known. However, the neutralization of fast and manoeuvrable small objects – tanks and other armoured or soft-skinned vehicles, as well as groups of mounted enemy troops – had been only partially resolved by the use of biplanes of older types – for example, the Heinkel He 51, or the Henschel Hs 123 (the initial Stuka) – as ground attack aircraft. As proven in Spain, these obsolescent airplanes were not fully suited to the task assigned to them, being rather slow, lightly armed and non-armoured, thus vulnerable to ground fire. The experience in the Spanish war theatre highlighted the need for a well protected and heavily armed specialized *Schlachtflugzeug* (ground attack aircraft). The existence of such a dedicated aircraft type was fully justified by the apparent necessities of the modern, fast-changing battlefield with flexible front lines, in contrast to the mostly fixed trench warfare, which characterized the 'Great War'.

Recognising early on the importance of the concept of close-support aircraft, which had been confirmed by experiences gained in the opening stage of the Spanish Civil War by the expeditionary *Legion Condor*, manned by German personnel, the *Technisches Amt* (Technical Bureau, LC or C-Amt) of the *Reichsluftfahrtministerium* (RLM, or the Reich's Air Ministry), issued a specification in April 1937, which addressed this particular topic. The directive called for a small, twin-engine aircraft, armed with a combination of 20 mm cannon and heavy machine guns, which also had to be capable of delivering a bomb load. The suggested, but not mandatory, powerplant was the pre-production Argus As 410 A-0. However, the performance of this in-line engine was less than ideal for this task. Although theoretically rated at 465 hp (346.7 Kw) for take-off, the actual power was only 430 hp (320.6 Kw) – rather underpowered for an all-metal heavily armed and armoured aircraft.

Since it was assumed that this new type of aircraft would operate at low-level over the battlefield, in areas where air supremacy had already been achieved, no rear defence armament was prescribed, albeit it was not clearly excluded either. Besides saving on manpower, the lack of a rear gunner

would also help to keep total weight down while allowing an increase in payload. However, proper armour protection for the pilot and engines from ground fire was considered crucial. Protection for the pilot in case of a forced landing was also regarded as important. Due to its intended role as a close support and ground-attack aircraft, the type was anticipated from the very beginning to operate from improvised airfields, close to the front line. Therefore, ruggedness and simplicity of the airframe construction, as well as easy maintenance and serviceability were paramount. No other requirements were formulated, the assigned companies being given a free hand to finalize the details.

The tender was issued to the following aircraft manufacturers: the Focke-Wulf *Flugzeugbau G.m.b.H.*, the Gothaer *Waggonfabrik A.G.*, the Hamburger *Flugzeugbau G.m.b.H.* and the Henschel *Flugzeug-Werke A.G.* By 1 October 1937 – the deadline set up by the C-Amt – Gotha had not submitted any proposals, while Focke-Wulf and Hamburger *Flugzeugbau* (which emerged as *Abteilung Flugzeugbau der Schiffswerft* Blohm & Voss during 1938) offered modified versions of their ongoing reconnaissance aircraft projects, the Fw 189 and Ha 141, respectively. Henschel was the only participating company to submit a totally new design, specifically developed to meet the requirements of the tender.

Design engineers at Hamburger *Flugzeugbau* planned to meet the *Schlachtflugzeug* requirements by modifying their existing Ha 141 type (later renamed BV 141). The project – an unconventional design – featuring an asymmetrical con-figuration, was tentatively allocated the designation Hamburg P 40. The single 1,050 hp Daimler-Benz DB 600 in-line engine

△ A Henschel Hs 129 B-2, 'Yellow G' belonging to II./Sch.G. 1 takes off. It was armed with a 30 mm MK 101 cannon under the fuselage, which first made its appearance in June 1942. Notice the unit emblem, an axe-wielding bear, painted just aft of the cockpit canopy. The black triangle, seen at left of the fuselage cross, denotes a ground attack aircraft.

△ This side view of the Hs 129's cockpit gives an indication of the confined space for the pilot. The padded leather windscreen frame helped avoid injury to the pilot's face/forehead in case of a crash landing. The pilot's seat has an extension, made of 6 mm armour plate, protecting him from an attack from the rear. Note the externally mounted Revi C/12C gun sight. The pilot is Hptm. Rudolf-Heinz Ruffer, one of the best and most successful of the Hs 129 pilots, with over 80 destroyed Soviet tanks to his credit.

▽ The pilot of this late production Hs 129 B-2 is helped by a member of the ground crew in being strapped into his seat. Note the short upturned exhaust tubes as fitted to late B-2 variants.

was mounted on the front of a single-boom fuselage, situated to the left of the aircraft's theoretical centreline, while the crew of two was housed in a separate nacelle offset to the right. Besides offering outstanding, all-round visibility for the crew, this unusual construction also presented a solution to the effect of propeller torque, present in every single-engine aircraft (for example, the well-known tendency of the Messerschmitt Bf 109 to swing during take-off and landings, the cause of frequent accidents).

Focke-Wulf's project was based on the Fw 189 reconnaissance aircraft, already under development. While the powerplants and twin-boom fuselage structure remained identical, the cockpit was reduced in size and heavily armoured. In contrast to the recce version, the number of crew was reduced from three to two – pilot and rear gunner – seated back-to-back. A 75 mm-thick armoured glass windscreen protected the pilot, while the gunner could look out through a narrow, rectangular, horizontal slot cut in the armoured nacelle. Armament would consist of a pair of forward firing 20 mm MG 151/20 cannon and a pair of 7.9 mm MG 17 machine guns, mounted in each side of the front fuselage. The rear gunner would operate a single 7.9 mm flexible machine gun.

Henschel's conventional design was apparently more suitable for its intended task. It was approximately 20 per cent smaller than the Focke-Wulf project – its main competitor – with a corresponding reduction in weight. Therefore, despite the identical Argus As 410 powerplants, the calculated top speed of Henschel's project was higher. Crew consisted of the pilot, no rear gunner being considered necessary. The truncated triangular fuselage cross section with rounded bottom was atypical, but it offered a small target. Moreover, the flat, angular fuselage sides were designed to deflect small-calibre projectiles coming from the ground. Besides being practical, the fuselage structure presented manufacturing advantages as well, although a disadvantage of the triangular fuselage was a rather cramped cockpit area. The truncated triangle cross-section was only 300 mm wide at the top, 1100 mm wide at the bottom and 1162 mm high. The fuselage top section width was actually dictated by an adult man's average shoulder width. Despite the pilot's rather confined area, the cockpit was ergonomically designed and met the basic requirements. The pilot's back was also well protected against projectiles coming from the rear – the Hs 129's most vulnerable area – by 6 mm thick armour plate that also doubled as the seat's back and adjustable head rest.

△ After being refuelled from an Opel fuel truck, this Hs 129 of 8.(Pz)/Sch.G 1 taxis to the take-off position. The wing fuel tanks of the Hs 129 B had a capacity of 205 litres.

In accordance with the original specification, the split, two-piece windscreen was made from armoured glass panels 75 mm thick – identical to that employed in the Focke-Wulf design. The cockpit's small side windows were also made of armour glass, albeit of lesser thickness than the windscreen. The steep, double-slanted nose offered excellent visibility of the ground ahead and below – a key element for the pilot of a low flying ground attack aircraft, requiring quick action against small, moving targets. Nevertheless, due to the restricted glass area, the pilot's visibility was considered quite poor – as was also the case with the Focke-Wulf design. The proposed armament was also identical to the Fw 189, except, for the aft-firing machine gun. The aiming device would consist of a Revi C/12C gunsight, placed outside, in front of the windscreen, as no room was left inside the cockpit. The design received the temporary Henschel designation P 46.

According to a Henschel document, the designers' goal was to create an aircraft of simple but effective construction, with reliable flying characteristics, emphasis being put on effective armament and pilot protection. They had hoped that the new Henschel design would be appreciated and beloved in the same way as the company's previous ground-attack aircraft, the Hs 123 biplane – popularly known as the 'Eins, Zwei, Drei' ('one-two-three') – was cherished by those who had flown it in peacetime and combat alike.

Following the initial assessment of the three entries, submitted on 1 October 1937, Hamburg's unorthodox concept was discarded from start by the C-Amt, leaving the Focke-Wulf's and Henschel designs in the final round. After representatives of the RLM's Technical Bureau thoroughly examined the wooden mock-ups and studied the estimated data submitted by the designers, they concluded that both the Focke-Wulf and Henschel proposals possessed advantages and disadvantages, and no clear winner had emerged by the end of the study period. Both projects were therefore accepted

△ Pilots of 8.(Pz)/Sch.G 1 pose at the tail of W.Nr. 0364 showing 13 'kill' markings. Ninth from the right is Lt. Hans-Hermann Steinkamp, who later became Staffelkapitän of 14.(Pz)/SG 9.

▽ An unidentified Schlachtflieger signals to a member of the ground crew his intention to take off. Note the white lines on the sliding cockpit perspex, indicating the dive angles. Visibility from the Hs 129 B's cockpit was excellent, except for the rear, which could be partially covered by the rear view mirror.

for further trials. This was not because the submissions were of equal merit, but because neither of them received the RLM's full approval, both being judged to be rather mediocre and barely meeting minimum requirements. The main problem was the unsuitable powerplant; as no medium-power German-built engine was available in numbers at that time. This deficiency would never be fully eliminated, and this would affect the would-be career of the *Luftwaffe's Schlachtflugzeug.*

In the early stage, it appears that Focke-Wulf's hybrid project was preferred over the Henschel original design. This was mainly due to the possibility of producing the reconnaissance version of the Fw 189 in parallel with the assault version, the powerplants and main structural parts – except for the cockpit – being identical. That would have allowed a larger number of aircraft to be built in a shorter time – an important advantage in view of the Third Reich's rapid rearmament plans of the late 1930s.

In September 1938, both companies received development contracts for three prototypes of each aircraft. The Focke-Wulf project did not receive a separate designation, as it was based on an already approved model, the 8-189 ('8' was the RLM prefix code for engine-powered aircraft), therefore the assault version was called Fw 189 S (S for *Schlacht,* or assault). In contrast, Henschel secured for his original design a new RLM List Number, 8-129, thus its ground-attack aircraft project became the Hs 129.

A true *Schlachtflugzeug* was born.

Prototypes and Pre-Series Production

"... nevertheless, it must be stressed that in contrast to the German test pilots comments, most German and Rumanian combat pilots who flew the series-produced Hs 129 B in actual combat conditions loved to fly it"

As soon as the RLM orders had been issued, preparation for production started at both the Focke-Wulf factory in Bremen and Henschel at their Schönefeld plant. Metal was cut in early October 1938, the initial prototypes – V1b for the Fw 189 and V1 for the Hs 129 – taking shape by the end of the year.

Since the Fw 189 V1 reconnaissance prototype had already been flying for several months when the RLM contract was secured, Focke-Wulf had a decisive timing advantage over Henschel. In late 1938, the Fw 189 V1 – *Werknummer* 1997, registered D-OPVN – was withdrawn from flight test and returned to the company's work shop for conversion to the assault role. The original extensively glazed cockpit was replaced with a new, much smaller and fully armoured design, while the rest of the aircraft's structure was left unchanged. Therefore, work on the revised Fw 189 V1a was completed quickly and the revised prototype flew for the first time in early 1939. However the initial results were rather unsatisfactory. The airframe was too heavy and visibility quite poor. Therefore, *Dipl.-Ing*. Kurt Tank, Focke-Wulf's chief designer, decided to redesign the nacelle, to overcome these deficiencies. The new sub-version was called the V1b.

Work at Henschel lagged behind. All efforts were focused to finish the all-new airframe as soon as possible, in order to catch up with the competition. By spring of 1939, the Hs 129 prototype was almost ready to fly, pending the availability of Argus engines and propellers. In accordance with the tradition existing at Henschel *Flugzeugwerk*, the V1 prototype received the first *Werknummer* (construction number) in the 3000 series, preceded by the aircraft's RLM List No., i.e., 129 3001 (it is interesting to note that the initial production number block assigned to the company's Hs 123 and Hs 126, as well as the license built Ju W34, Ju 86 and Ju 88, always started with '3001'). However, delivery of the Argus engines and propellers were delayed several times and this, naturally, also delayed the actual date of the Hs 129 V1's first flight.

Even before either of the prototypes could leave the ground, the RLM drew up plans based on the new generation of ground-attack aircraft. Production Plan No. 10, issued in December 1938, called again – nineteen months after the previous Plan – for *Schlachtflugzeuge* to be delivered to the *Luftwaffe* as soon as possible. While in April 1937 the assault aircraft listed in the previous Plan was still the Henschel Hs 123 biplane, by December 1938 this had been changed to the Fw 189 S. The Plan envisaged 102 Focke-Wulfs to be built between 1 January 1939 and 30 June 1941. The next Plan, No. 11, to run from 1 April 1939 to 1 April 1942, retained the Fw 189 S as the aircraft of choice, the total number being increased to 225.

On 5 August 1939, a special high-level meeting took place with the participation of senior *Luftwaffe* officials. *Reichsluftfahrtminister* (Reich's Minister of Air) Hermann

△ The Fw 189 V1 was rebuilt to compete with the Hs 129 as a heavily armed ground-support aircraft. This early adaptation, retaining the code D-OPVN, first flew in the spring of 1939 and was powered by two Argus AS 410 engines, but its performance was disappointing. In 1940, the V6 was also converted into a ground attack aircraft.

Göring proposed a shift in aircraft production to single-engine fighters and multi-engine bombers at the expense of other types such as assault aircraft. By now, the latter category was represented in the RLM's plans by both the Fw 189 and the Hs 129. This was the first time the Henschel product was officially listed in an RLM Delivery Plan. Nevertheless, the RLM Technical Office Production Programme No. 16, issued on 25 October 1939, still listed the Fw 189 – without the actual sub-type being given – as the *Luftwaffe's* main assault aircraft of choice. Total production was increased once again, to about 400. However, not a single aircraft had been accepted for *Luftwaffe* service. This was because the results of the official flight tests had not yielded the expected results.

△ The original Fw 189 V1 had its cockpit modified with more armour protection and was given the designation Fw 189 V1a and V1b. The aircraft was written off in an accident caused by the pilot's poor visibility from the cockpit. The Argus engines also retained the two-bladed fixed propellers from the original prototype but two yellow bands were painted around the fuselage to denote the modification. Two different canopies, designated V1a and V1b, were experimented with. There was a third modification designated the V1c.

▷ The eventual winner of the RLM's Schlachtflugzeug tender, issued in April 1937, was the twin-engine Henschel Hs 129 – the sole participant designed for the purpose of the ground-attack role. Depicted is the Hs 129 V-1 (D-ONUD, W.Nr. 129 3001), finished in overall RLM 63, light grey in May 1939, prior to its maiden flight. It was later repainted in the greens RLM 70/ 71 over RLM 65 light blue and received the Stammkennzeichen (Radio Call Sign) TF+AM painted in black.

△ This front view of the Hs 129 V-1 clearly shows the details of the Argus As 410 in-line engines fitted with two-bladed fixed pitch propellers. Note the slanted, pointed nose, the three-segmented windscreen and short gun channels. Note also the two long, continuous bomb racks fitted under the front section of the fuselage. These details would all be changed in the upcoming pre-series aircraft.

△ This photograph clearly illustrates the crude construction and general appearance of the modified armoured cockpit of a Hs 129 prototype. The pilot's forward visibility - already severely restricted by the small two piece armoured windscreen and the vertically split thick frame - was further obscured by the externally mounted gun-sight.

The light grey painted Hs 129 V1 – carrying the civil code D-ONUD – took off on its maiden flight on 26 May 1939, from the airfield at Schönefeld – a few weeks after the Focke-Wulf Fw 189 V1b's first flight. The experienced test pilot's first impressions however were damning. As with the Fw 189 V1b, tested earlier, complaints concerned the poor forward visibility as well as to the sides, only average handling characteristics and low engine power. The two competing prototypes also had further different drawbacks. While the Henschel Hs 129 suffered from a severely cramped cockpit, the Focke-Wulf design suffered from a higher overall weight, which further diminished the already inadequate manoeuvrability. With the extensive flight trials in progress, the balance began to tip slightly in favour of the Henschel design.

A further setback for Focke-Wulf was the crash landing of the V1b, due to poor visibility! Focke-Wulf used this unexpected setback to recall the prototype and carry out improvements. The fuselage nacelle was redesigned, visibility improved and the crew reduced to just the pilot. This was in accordance with modified RLM requirements, which stated that besides which engine type was to be used, that the airframe was to be for a single-seat, low-wing aircraft. Henschel's design also possibly had an influence on the development work at Focke-Wulf. In the autumn, the modified V1b returned to *Erprobungsstelle* (Test Centre, abbreviated as E-Stelle) Rechlin. Shortly thereafter, it again force-landed, after both rudders were lost in a test flight on 8 November 1939 (the Hs 129 V1 was transferred to Rechlin

△ **The nose of an Hs 129 A-0 showing the cockpit and bomb-sight.**
1 – The Revi C/12C bomb-sight
2 – Target line of sight

only on 14 December). After being repaired, it was modified yet again and the new sub-version being designated the V1c.

In the meantime, the Hs 129 V2 (W.Nr. 129 3002) had been completed at Schönefeld and had taken to the air on 30 November 1939. This second prototype did not last long, as it was destroyed during a test flight on 5 January 1940, when it failed to recover from a dive. The Hs 129 V2 was followed by the V3 (W.Nr. 129 3003). The maiden flight was again delayed due to the unavailability of the engines and propellers. Subsquently the V3 was first flown on 2 April 1940. The V3 then joined the V1 at *E-Stelle* Rechlin. In the meantime the V1 had received the *Stammkennzeichen* (Radio Call Sign) TF+AM, a system introduced from 18 October 1939 onwards. V3 became TF+AO. A situation report by *C-Amt*, dated 1 September 1940, listed the Hs 129 V1 as being under *'allgemeine Erprobung'* (general test) at Rechlin, the V2 (assigned with code TF+AN, but not used) written off in a previous crash, while the V3 (TF+AO) was being returned to Henschel's Schönefeld works for repair due to an earlier accident.

During the same month, the improved Focke-Wulf model, the Fw 189 V6 (W.Nr. 0016, code D-OGAB, later coded NA+WB), arrived at the Rechlin Test Centre for further comparison trials. This was a futile exercise, however, as the RLM's preference had by then decisively shifted towards the Henschel aircraft, because of final modifications, which were either already implemented or were promised for the near future. A further convincing factor in favour of the Henschel design were the production costs, envisaged as being two-thirds of that calculated by Focke-Wulf. The importance of the Fw 189 S – since renamed Fw 189 C – therefore diminished and it was now considered only as a reserve, in case the Hs 129 proved a total failure. The RLM's still unofficial decision was already reflected in the next Production Plan, where the Hs 129 traded place with the Fw 189 C. The latter type appeared for the last time in the *C-Amt's* Production Programme, dated 1 July 1940, with only 60 units to be delivered by October 1940, when production was to be stopped. Focke-Wulf still assigned 11 C-Os to the *Schlachtflugzeug* programme (W.Nr. 0017-0027) and planned for 60 Fw 189 C-1s.

Parallel to the ongoing evaluation and operational tests in July 1940, Henschel started the production of twenty-three A-0 pre-series aircraft, ordered by the RLM. Production was to be completed by November 1940. These airframes were tentatively assigned the Werknummer batch 129 3004 to 129 3026. The first A-0 received the *Luftwaffe* radio call sign GM+OA, the remaining A-0s being assigned with the rest of the code sequence. The maiden flight of the first A-0 took place on 1 August 1940. In September 1940, the RLM reduced the number of A-0s to 12 (W.Nr. 129 3004–129 3015, GM+OA to GM+OL), while the additionally ordered 16 A-1s were to be refitted with more powerful engines and subsequently assigned with a new pre-series sub-type, the B-0. The balance from the reduced A-0 pre-series batch –11 aircraft– was included into the improved new sub-type, the B-0, increasing the total number from 16 to 27 aircraft. This latter

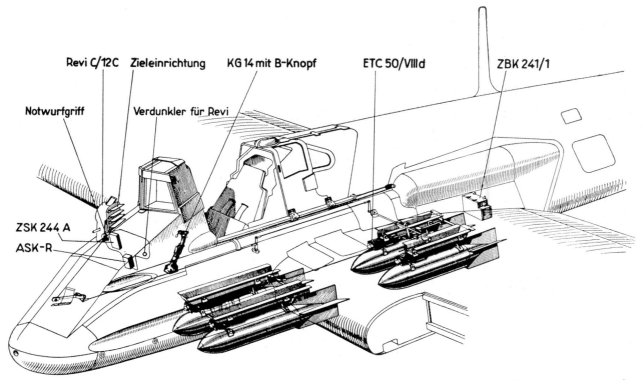

Revi C/12C   Zieleinrichtung   KG 14 mit B-Knopf   ETC 50/VIIId   ZBK 241/1

Notwurfgriff   Verdunkler für Revi

ZSK 244 A
ASK-R

Abb. 1: Anordnung der Abwurfwaffen in der Hs 129 ~~A und B~~
A-0

5   7   6   3

4   1   2

△ Details of bomb dropping equipment for the Hs 129 A-0 as described in handbook L.Dv.T.2129 A-0/B-0 dated February 1941. Bomb-carrying capacity was 4 X SC 50 or 4 X SD 50. Alternatively, four racks of BdC10 anti-personnel bombs with 5 X C10 bombs could be carried on each rack. Note the annotation 'A-0' in pen to the title of the drawing - written in the original handbook during the war.

◁ **Hs 129 A-0 cockpit interior indicating bomb release instruments.**
1 – Bomb release button
2 – Emergency release handle
3 – Selection switch grip
4 – Bomb primer indicator for each ETC 50/VIIId bomb rack
5 – Turn button to darken bomb-sight
6 – Handle for covering the pilot's right-hand windscreen panel with a shade.

batch received a new *Werknummer* block, 0016 to 0042 instead of 129 3016 to 129 3042, and was planned to be delivered between February to May 1941. This deadline could not be kept, however, as the last A-0 only rolled off the production line in May 1941. Eventually, the B-0 pre-series was completed in early 1942 – after a delay of almost a year.

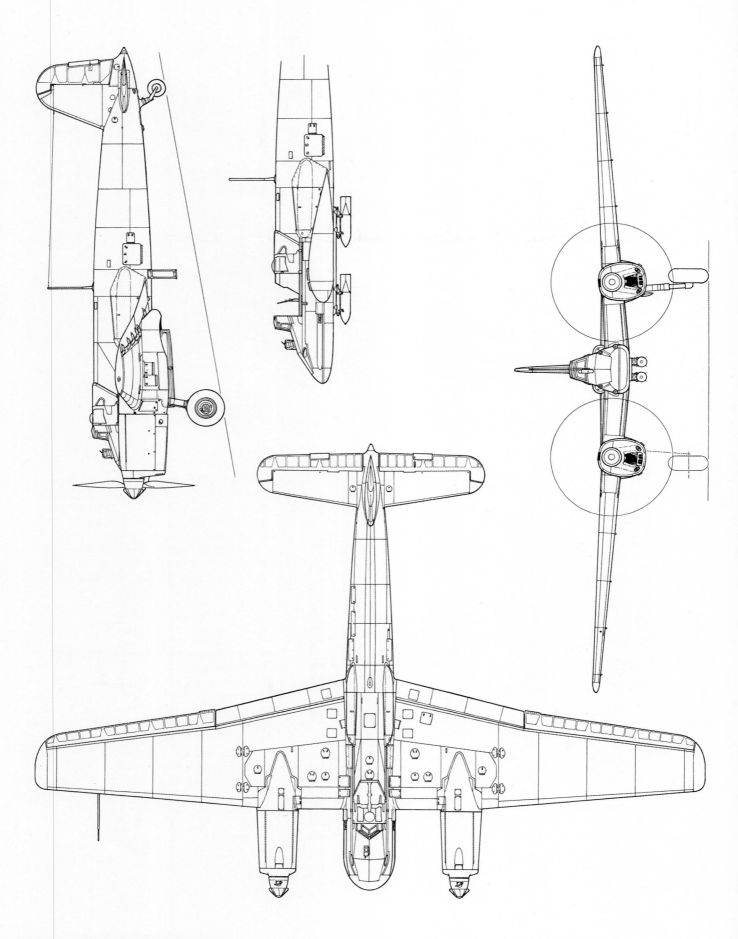

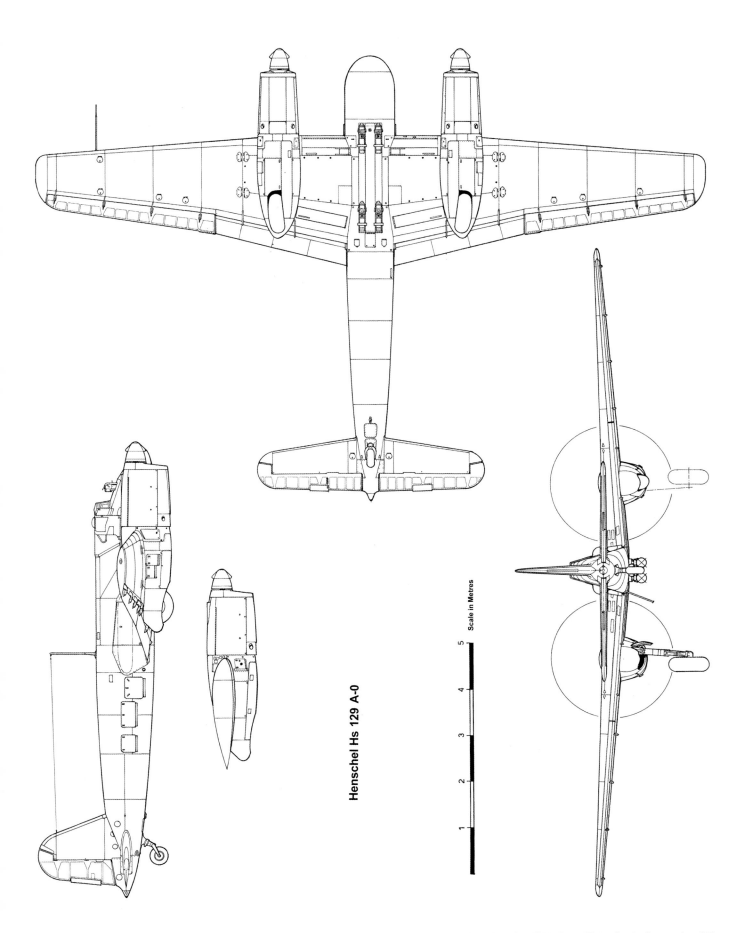

Henschel Hs 129 A-0

Scale in Metres

1 2 3 4 5

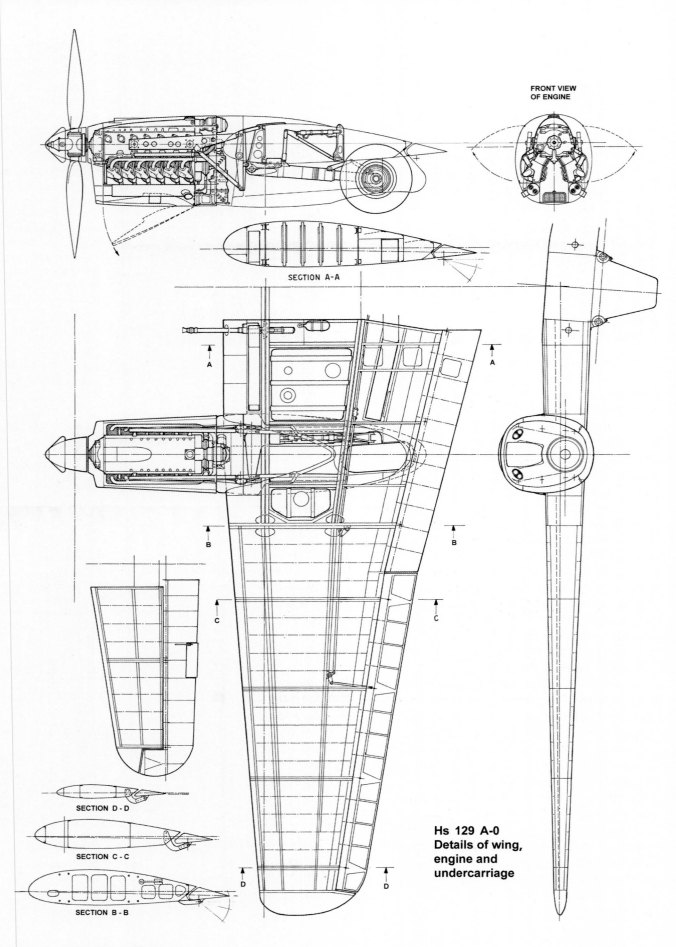

FRONT VIEW
OF ENGINE

SECTION A-A

SECTION D - D

SECTION C - C

SECTION B - B

Hs 129 A-0
Details of wing,
engine and
undercarriage

In the autumn of 1940, the first completed A-0s were delivered to a specialist unit, namely the 5. *(Schlacht) Staffel* (5th Ground Attack Squadron) of *Lehrgeschwader* 2 (LG 2, or the 2nd Operational Development Wing), based at Tutow, for trials under service conditions. At that time, the unit was equipped with Hs 123 biplanes and Bf 109 E monoplanes. Seven Hs 129 A-0s were taken in charge by the end of the year. Seasoned test pilots were far from satisfied with the Hs 129 A. Despite the improvements already implemented by Henschel, the main complaints remained the same as previously mentioned by the E-Stelle test pilots: poor visibility, low engine power and average handling characteristics. Before the year's end, the first fatality had already occurred, when Hs 129 A-0, W.Nr. 3009 (GM+OF), flown by *Feldwebel* (Technical Sergeant) *Dipl.-Ing.* Hermann Balke, crashed fatally at Braunschweig on 16 December, killing an unidentified mechanic on the ground, while a second mechanic was injured. Despite this tragedy, the test programme continued, as the *Luftwaffe*, heading towards an all-out confrontation, badly needed a dedicated ground-support aircraft as soon as possible.

In early 1941, the ongoing order had been changed, yet again, by the RLM. The new request called for 60 Hs 129 A-1/14M – instead of the 60 Fw 189 Cs, strangely ordered on 1 July 1940, which had now been over-ridden. The suffix after the Hs 129's sub-type designation represented the type of replacement powerplant finally settled upon by the RLM – namely the Gnome-Rhône 14M 04/05 radial. The French engine was rated at 700 hp (522 kW) the maximum take-off power at 3030 RPM (revolutions per minute), which represented a welcome 50 per cent increase compared to the earlier Argus in-line engine. The chosen powerplant was nevertheless considered an intermediary one, until the Argus or BMW (Bramo) companies were able to develop a new, medium-power engine with over 1000 hp (745.7 kW) output. This new, superior engine would eventually power the *Schlachtflugzeug* in the anticipated mass production. This, of

△ A photograph of Hs 129 A-0, W.Nr. 3005, White 5 coded GM+OB, was one of 12 pre-production series A-0s used by the Luftwaffe to train pilots in the ground-attack role. This aircraft flew with the Ergänzungszerstörergruppe until it was destroyed at Deblin-Irena, Poland, on 19 June 1942.

△ A belly-landed Hs 129 A-0 "Red 16" belonging to SG 101 based at Paris-Orly. The Infanterie-sturmabzeichen marking on the nose was also used by the training flights.

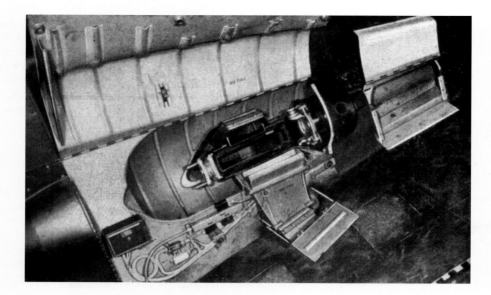

◁ Details of the cover panels for the MG 151 installed in the side of the fuselage of the Hs 129 A-0. The design of these panels were later modified on the B series.

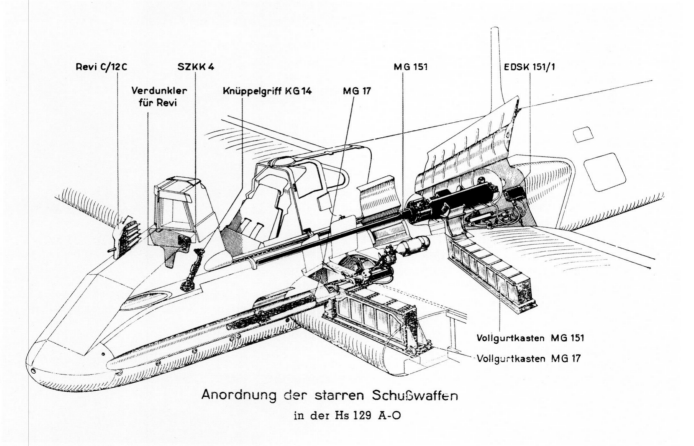

Revi C/12C   SZKK 4   MG 151   EDSK 151/1

Verdunkler für Revi   Knüppelgriff KG 14   MG 17

Vollgurtkasten MG 151

Vollgurtkasten MG 17

Anordnung der starren Schußwaffen
in der Hs 129 A-O

△ After the initial proposal to configure the Hs 129 A-0 to be fitted with bombs, a further handbook, L.Dv.T.2129 A-0/Wa, issued in March 1941, detailed the armament fitted in both sides of the fuselage.

course, never actually happened, and the Hs 129 retained the problematic and somewhat weak French powerplant throughout its production life, which affected the actual combat efficiency of the aircraft. Nevertheless, it must be stressed that in contrast to the exigent of German test pilots, most German and Rumanian combat pilots who flew the series produced Hs 129 B in actual combat conditions *loved* to fly it, although more powerful and reliable powerplants would certainly have had a positive impact on the type's overall performance.

◁ Following the acceptance of the Hs 129 project by the RLM, Henschel Flugzeugwerk received an order for three prototypes in September 1938, followed by another order calling for 23 pre-production series A-0s (later reduced to 12). The Hs 129 A-0 was powered by a pair of Argus As 410 in-line engines, which gave a characteristic shape to the pre-series aircraft. GM+OJ was the tenth 'Anton' and the thirteenth Hs 129 airframe built (W.Nr. 129 3013).

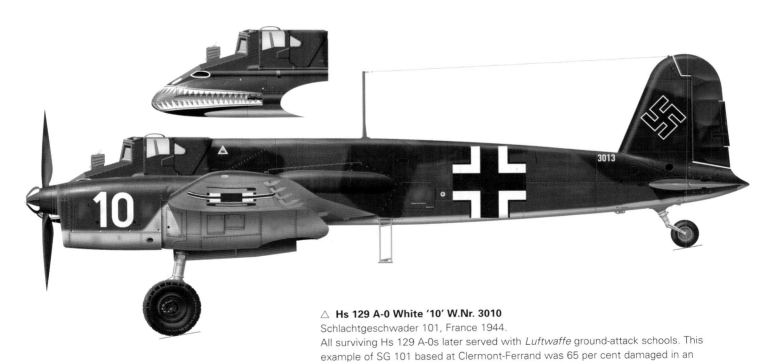

△ Hs 129 A-0 White '10' W.Nr. 3010

Schlachtgeschwader 101, France 1944.

All surviving Hs 129 A-0s later served with *Luftwaffe* ground-attack schools. This example of SG 101 based at Clermont-Ferrand was 65 per cent damaged in an Allied bombing attack on 30 April 1944. Note the large pike's mouth marking painted on the nose. This feature was intended to enhance the shape of the nose as a recognition aid and a German recognition publication of the period describes the nose area as '...like a pike's head'.

B-1: The Greatly Improved 'Berta'

"... the cockpit enclosure was completely redesigned. To significantly improve the pilot's view, the earlier, V-shaped, two-piece windscreen was changed to an enlarged, slightly curved, single piece unit."

△ A photograph taken after a successful test flight at the Henschel works shows, from left to right: Dipl.Ing. Carl Frydag, Henschel works director; Flugkapitän Ing. Hans Wilhelm Kaempf, Chief Test Pilot, who was later killed testing the Hs 130 E-0 V2 high-altitude aircraft, when it crashed due to an engine fire; Herr Regelin, Head of the Design Office and Dipl.Ing. Friedrich Nicolaus, Chief Design Engineer.

After the operational trials were completed and the findings drawn up, the RLM refused to accept the A-1 sub-variant for mass production due to its still sluggish performance, despite most changes required by the test pilots having been incorporated in the improved design. Besides the new powerplant, a completely modified airframe was now requested as well, which was hoped to result in significantly improved qualities. Accordingly, Henschel's chief designer, Dipl.-Ing. Friedrich Nicolaus, started a new project based on the A-1. This project, the Henschel P 76, retained the same configuration, but called for enlarged overall dimensions. The wingspan was increased to 15.50 m, the fuselage length to 10.11 m and the height to 3.51 m. The enlarged airframe was to be powered by a pair of French Gnome-Rhône 14M 04/05 radial engines, driving a three-blade Ratier variable pitch metal propeller. Concomitantly, however, the overall weight would have increased by a similar percentage to the size enlargement, reducing the advantage gained from the larger airframe.

The pressing need for a ground-attack aircraft to be ready for the pending conflict persuaded the RLM to cancel the new project, which would have required a further year's work to be finalised. Instead, Henschel *Flugzeugwerk A. G.* was ordered to adapt the existing Hs 129 A-1 airframes to accommodate the selected new French powerplant. The upgraded cockpit design had to be included in the new design as well, as it significantly increased the pilot's all-around visibility, clearing one of the main complaints of the test pilots. Except for the ten A-1s already in manufacture, the rest of the initial order calling for 60 airframes was – temporarily – suspended. However, the RLM reassured Henschel that once field tests with the re-engined and improved airframe demonstrated that the requirements had been met, the order would be promptly reinstated. Accordingly, Henschel selected the ten existing modified A-1/14Ms to be fitted with the Gnome-Rhône 14M radial engines, as planned. The counter-clockwise rotating 14M 04 radial was fitted to port, while the clockwise rotating 14M 05 radial was fitted to starboard. These aircraft were renamed B-1s, but kept their original batch of construction numbers (0151-0160). They were allocated with a new block of *Stammkennzeichen*, starting at KG+GI. They were to be delivered by early 1942. In accordance with this decision, the RLM Programme dated 1 January 1941 still called for 60 Hs 129 B variants – the pending order – powered by Gnome-Rhône 14M radials, to be delivered between June and December. The previous order calling for the 16 + 11 original Argus-powered A-1s was maintained; however, the airframes were to be re-engined with the Gnome-Rhône 14M radials. The new batch – now renamed B-0s – were assigned with *Stammkennzeichen* starting at KK+VI, and W.Nr. 0016 to 0042.

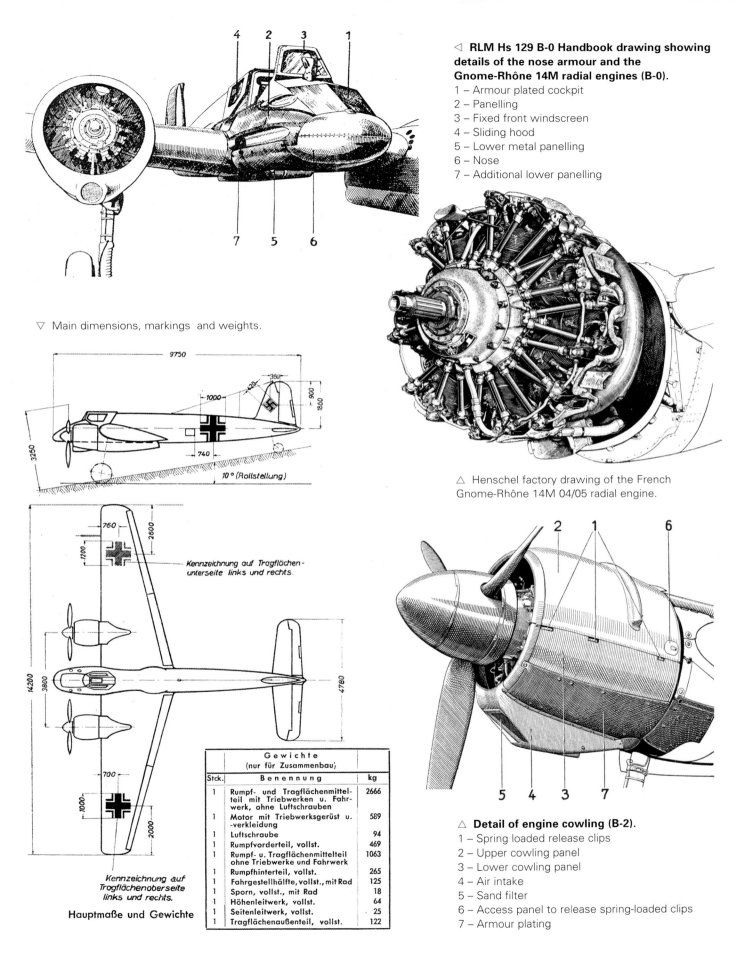

◁ **RLM Hs 129 B-0 Handbook drawing showing details of the nose armour and the Gnome-Rhône 14M radial engines (B-0).**
1 – Armour plated cockpit
2 – Panelling
3 – Fixed front windscreen
4 – Sliding hood
5 – Lower metal panelling
6 – Nose
7 – Additional lower panelling

▽ Main dimensions, markings and weights.

10° (Rollstellung)

Kennzeichnung auf Tragflächen-
unterseite links und rechts.

Kennzeichnung auf
Tragflächenoberseite
links und rechts.

Hauptmaße und Gewichte

△ Henschel factory drawing of the French Gnome-Rhône 14M 04/05 radial engine.

Gewichte (nur für Zusammenbau)		
Stck.	Benennung	kg
1	Rumpf- und Tragflächenmittel-teil mit Triebwerken u. Fahr-werk, ohne Luftschrauben	2666
1	Motor mit Triebwerksgerüst u. -verkleidung	589
1	Luftschraube	94
1	Rumpfvorderteil, vollst.	469
1	Rumpf- u. Tragflächenmittelteil ohne Triebwerke und Fahrwerk	1063
1	Rumpfhinterteil, vollst.	265
1	Fahrgestellhälfte, vollst., mit Rad	125
1	Sporn, vollst., mit Rad	18
1	Höhenleitwerk, vollst.	64
1	Seitenleitwerk, vollst.	25
1	Tragflächenaußenteil, vollst.	122

△ **Detail of engine cowling (B-2).**
1 – Spring loaded release clips
2 – Upper cowling panel
3 – Lower cowling panel
4 – Air intake
5 – Sand filter
6 – Access panel to release spring-loaded clips
7 – Armour plating

▷ A contrived photograph reproduced from a war-time German aircraft recognition manual showing an early Hs 129 B-0, coded KK+VP W.Nr. 0023.

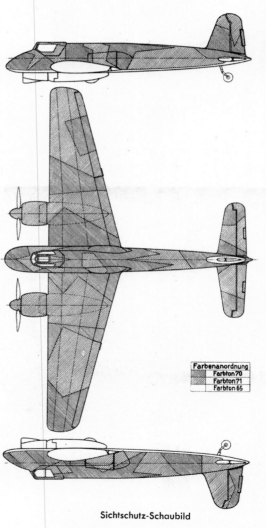

Sichtschutz-Schaubild

Farbenanordnung	
	Farbton 70
	Farbton 71
	Farbton 65

△ Factory standard camouflage pattern. (RLM 70, 71, 65 colours).

The first airframe actually to be re-engined with the French radial was the V3 prototype (W.Nr. 129 3003), still under tests at *E-Stelle* Rechlin. On 1 February 1941, it was pulled back to the Henschel Schönefeld works, where the wing centre section and engine bearers were extensively modified to accommodate the larger and heavier air-cooled radial engine. Some internal equipment was relocated towards the tail to compensate for the shift in the centre of gravity displaced forward, caused by the heavier engines. The fuselage was left almost untouched, except for small modifications. The prototype now renamed Hs 129 V3/U1 (U for *Umbausatz*, or conversion kit) performed its maiden flight on 19 March 1941. As expected, the more powerful radials did significantly improve the Hs 129's overall performance. Trials at Rechlin confirmed the evolution, the test pilots giving a more enthusiastic reaction to the new Hs 129 V3. This gave a green light to start modifying all existing airframes to the new 'B' standard.

As a step to optimizing manufacture, the wing leading edge was straightened and the trailing edge also followed a straight, tapering line. As a consequence, wing surface increased slightly, from 28.40 square metres to 29.00 square metres. The fuselage nose was enlarged and slightly rounded, offering an aerodynamically cleaner profile. The cockpit enclosure was completely redesigned. To significantly improve the pilot's view, the earlier, V-shaped, two-piece windscreen was changed to an enlarged, slightly curved, single piece unit. The area of the side glass panels was doubled and was modified to allow them to be opened and to slide rearwards, allowing the pilot to reach out, if needed. Additionally, the cabin's previous metal top panel was partially replaced with an armoured glass panel, which improved the pilot's upward visibility. It was probably at this stage that several engine instrument gauges were moved from

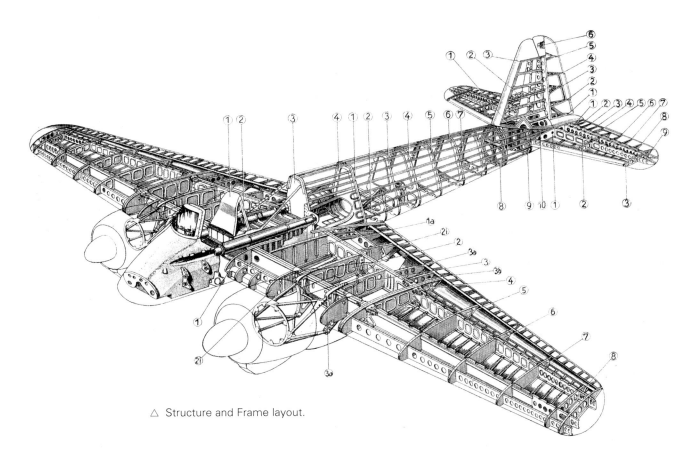

△ Structure and Frame layout.

△ An unusual view of the sixth Hs 129 B-0, coded KK+VN taken on the hard-standing at the Henschel Flugzeugwerk in late 1941. All the main features of the new sub-type can be clearly discerned from this factory photograph. The aircraft's Werknummer, 0021, was painted in white on the rear fuselage spine which was typical to all A-0, B-0 and B-1 sub-types. Interestingly, the wing and horizontal stabilizers on the upper surfaces were crudely overpainted in an unidentified colour, slightly lighter in appearance to the standard RLM 71, Dark Green.

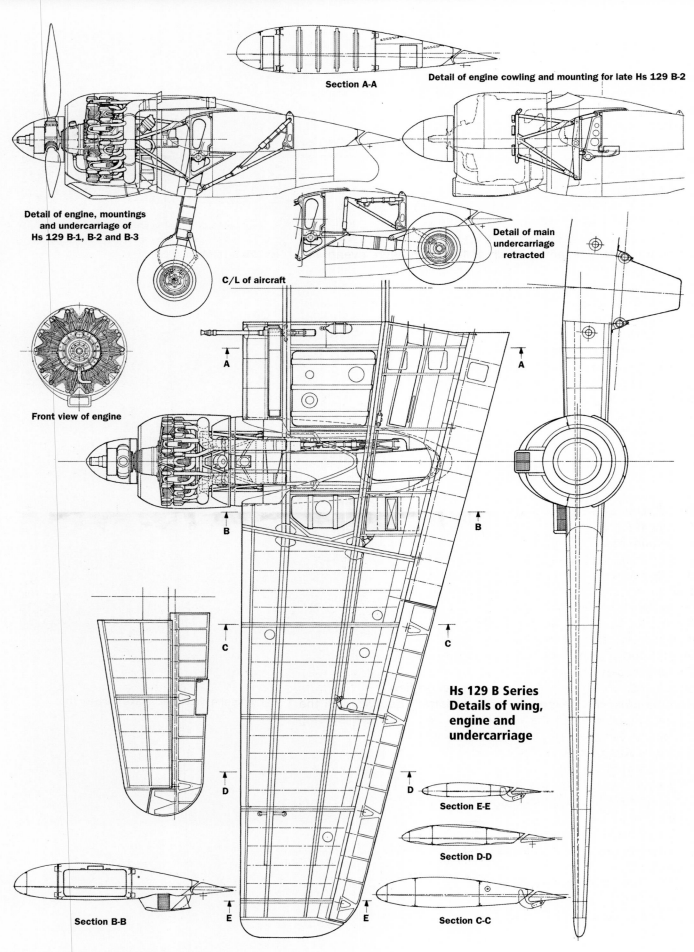

Section A-A

Detail of engine cowling and mounting for late Hs 129 B-2

Detail of engine, mountings and undercarriage of Hs 129 B-1, B-2 and B-3

Detail of main undercarriage retracted

C/L of aircraft

Front view of engine

Hs 129 B Series Details of wing, engine and undercarriage

Section E-E

Section D-D

Section C-C

Section B-B

the over-cramped cockpit panel out to the inner part of the engine cowlings, allowing the pilot to monitor them by looking through the now larger side windows. With all these modifications completed, it can be stated that the end result – the Hs 129 *'Berta'* – was a significantly better machine than its predecessor, the *'Anton'*. The first complete aircraft to be modified to test the improvements incorporated into the B-0 series was Hs 129 A-0, W.Nr. 129 3007, GM+OD. Production of the B-0 started in the last month of 1940. Despite the highest priority being given to the new sub-variant, the first true B-0, W.Nr. 0016, KK+VI, did not roll off the production line until August 1941 due to the changed powerplant and the afore-mentioned modifications. The second and third B-0s followed the next month. The entire batch of 18 aircraft were eventually only completed in early 1942. Even before the final B-0 rolled off the production line, the first fatal accident had occurred. The second B-0, W.Nr. 0017, KK+VJ, belonging to Henschel *Flugzeugwerk* Department E7, crashed in the hands of test pilot *Fw.* Konrad Bewermeyer on 6 January, during trials at *Erprobungsstelle* Rechlin.

△ A photograph taken from a wartime instructional training slide of one of the first Hs 129 B-1s, W.Nr. 0152, KG+GJ.

Luckily, it was to be the only such catastrophe that occurred during test flights of the new sub-type, the *'Berta'*. W.Nr. 0039 and 0042 were flown, repeatedly by *Gefr.* Siegfried Schuricht, a pilot in III./*Zerstörerschule* 2 on Tatsinskaya airfield, Soviet Union, in July and August 1942.

Considerable confusion exists when discussing the Hs 129's standard armament and various weapon kits, generally known as *Rüstsatz*. An RLM GL/C-B2 [a de-nomination that can be broken down, as follows: *General-luftzeugmeister* (GL), *Technisches Amt* (C), *Fliegerische Gerät* (B), *Flugzeuge* (2)], document, dated 1 January 1942, classified as *Geheime Kommandosache* (Secret Command Matter), dealing with the available weapons for the Hs 129 B-1, mentions the following armament variations:

△ Another image taken from a wartime instruction training slide of a Hs 129 B-2, W.Nr.0202, GD+ZB. This aircraft started life as a B-1 (note the circular air intake beneath the engine). The first ten B-2 airframes were B-1s, upgraded to B-2 standards.

Ständige Ausrüstung (Standard, or Permanently Used Equipment):

2 x 7.92 mm MG 17 machine guns, with 1000 rounds each (firing forward, mounted on each side of the fuselage centre section),

2 x 20 mm MG 151 cannon, with 250 rounds each (firing forward, mounted on each side of the fuselage centre section),

2 x 50 kg C50 or 48 x SD2 2.2 kg bombs (attached under the wings),

1 *Robot* (Automatic Camera) 24 x 24, with 60 frames.

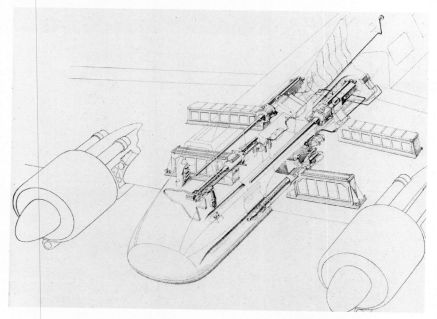

▽ RLM layout drawing of the standard armament of 2 X MG 17s and 2 X MG 151s as installed in the sides of the fuselage centre section.

Zusätzliche Ausrüstung (Auxiliary Equipment):

1 x 30 mm MK 101 cannon, with 30 rounds (mounted under fuselage in a streamlined gondola), or

4 x 7.92 mm MG 17 machine guns, with 1000 rounds each (same location, similar protective cover), or

4 x 50 kg C50 or 1 x 250 kg C250 or 96 x SD2 kg bombs (attached to under-fuselage rack), or

1 Rb 20/30 (Automatic Camera).

No official word on any particular numeric *Rüstsatz* designation – widely used with other *Luftwaffe* aircraft – is given. The RLM *Lieferpläne* (or Delivery Plans), again, do not mention any particular *Rüstsatz* designations, only the available armament and equipment variations. The numerically identified *Rüstsatz* armament sets could only be found in a few official factory-issued general coverage manuals for the Hs 129 B (see the aircraft's technical sheet); however, most of the detailed technical manuals prefer to spell out the specific combinations, without attaching a particular number. Therefore, the author has decided to avoid the use of any particular numeric *Rüstsatz* designations, preferring to describe the individual weapon and equipment kits, according to original available German documents.

Once the improvements and viability of the weapons were confirmed in field tests, the RLM – despite continuing reluctance – finally gave acceptance to the revised Hs 129 B-1. Simultaneously, high priority was also given to series production.

As mentioned before, the first main series airframes changed to the new 'B' standards were the 27 A-1s (W.Nr. 0016-0042) already under production, which were renamed B-0s. Next on the production line were the ten initial B-0s (W.Nr. 0151-0160), also under construction, now upgraded to the B-1 standard. These were to be followed by 50 planned B-1s (W.Nr. 0161-0210), which concluded the B-1 series. This number would also fulfil the existing RLM order calling for 60 improved *Schlachtflugzeuge*. However, only the first 40 airframes were eventually completed as B-1 (W.Nr. 0161-0200), as the last ten were upgraded to the new B-2 standard. The 50th and last B-1 (W.Nr. 0200) rolled off the production line in mid-May 1942. By then, production shifted from Schönefeld, the main centre to the Henschel *Flugzeugwerk* Johannisthal works, where aircraft production at HFW originally started in 1933, in the facilities of a bankrupt car manufacturer where mass production was planned.

Even before the first series B-1 was handed over, the RLM had issued a new purchase order on 15 October 1941. Initially,

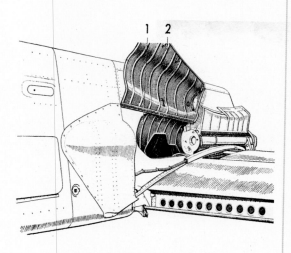

△ **Detail of the panelling of the fuselage centre section.**
1 – Trough for MG 151
2 – Cover plate for MG 151

▽ Four photographs showing the installation sequence for the 20 mm MG 151 cannon.

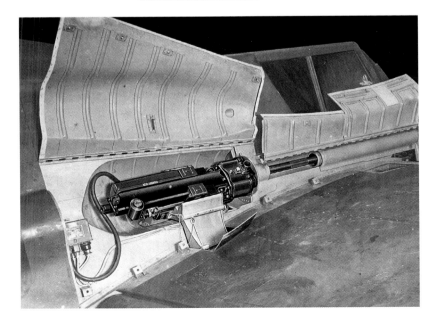

▷ An armourer fills an ammunition tray with shells for the MG 151/20 cannon prior to installation in the wing of an Hs 129.

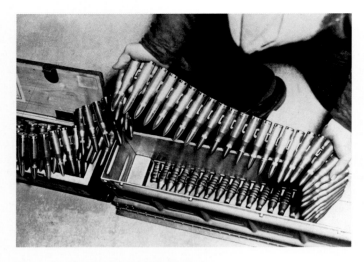

△▷ An armourer of 10.(Pz)/SG 9 installs a 125-round ammunition belt into a starboard side-mounted MG 151/20. Luftwaffe mechanics were nicknamed 'blackmen' because of the colour of their standard issue padded overalls. This airman is also wearing sheepskin-lined and padded headgear and gloves for protection against the severity of the Russian winter.

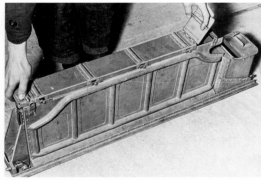

△ The ammunition container for the 7.92 mm calibre MG 17 machine gun being made ready for installation into the inner wing section. Each container carried 1,000 rounds of ammunition.

◁ An armourer installing an MG 17 machine gun into the starboard wing root and fuselage position of an Hs 129.

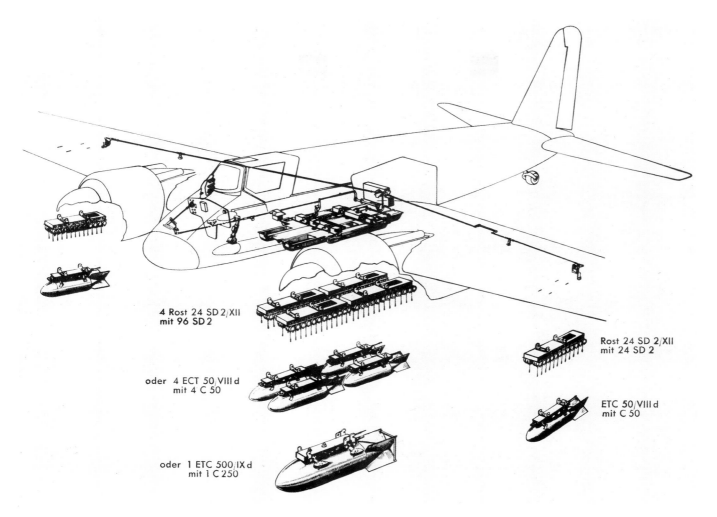

4 Rost 24 SD 2/XII
mit 96 SD 2

oder 4 ECT 50/VIII d
mit 4 C 50

oder 1 ETC 500/IX d
mit 1 C 250

Rost 24 SD 2/XII
mit 24 SD 2

ETC 50/VIII d
mit C 50

△ An RLM drawing showing the various bomb-load configurations applicable to the Hs 129 B-1 and B-2.

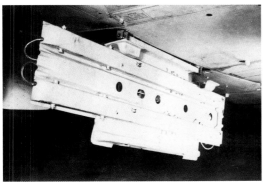

△▷ The ETC bomb carrier tray fitted with four 4 X ETC 50 VIIId bomb shackles showing some of the wiring leading to the bomb control panel in the cockpit. With the panel fitted and bomb carrier panel fixed in the horizontal position, four SC 50 bombs could be attached to each bomb carrier and connected to the electrical fuzing arm.

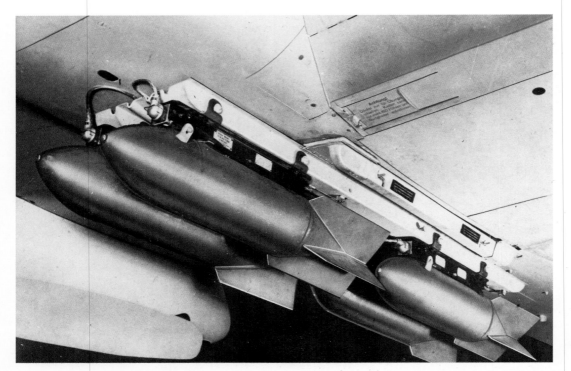

◁ The standard ETC bomb carrier fitted with four SC50 bombs. In addition a single SC50 bomb could also be fitted under each wing on an ETC 50 VIIId carrier.

◁ An operational Hs 129 B-1 fitted with 6 x SC50 bombs.

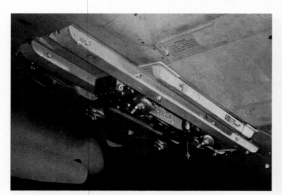

△▷ The ETC bomb carrier configured to carry a single SC250 bomb. This configuration was rarely used by the Luftwaffe.

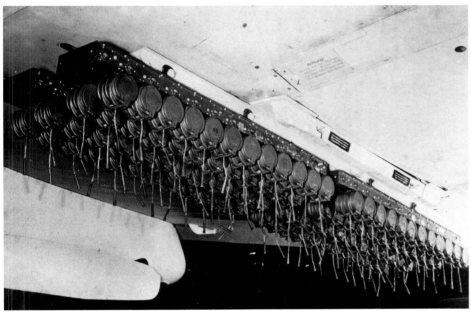

◁▽ Two views of the standard ETC bomb carrier tray fitted with four SD 2 XII bomb racks, which were capable of carrying 24 anti-personnel bombs, each weighing 2.2 kg (4.8 lbs).

the order called for 250 tropicalised Hs 129 B-1s (W.Nr. 0201-0450). However, in April 1942 this modification was dropped and the actual specification changed to a new and further improved sub-type, the B-2, with an option of up to 1000 additional aircraft. Although the B-2 was to be powered by the same readily available Gnome-Rhône 14M engines (because the series-produced Hs 129s still did not fully meet requirements) the RLM requested that from W.Nr. 0450 onwards, a new, more powerful and reliable, yet unspecified, engine type should be fitted to the unchanged airframes.

Despite the urgency given to the *Schlachtflugzeug* programme, on 22 June 1941 – the date of the commencement of the attack on the Soviet Union – the *Luftwaffe* order of battle did not list a single dedicated *Schlachtflugzeug* (compared to the 51 such aircraft – Hs 123s – existing on 10 May 1940).

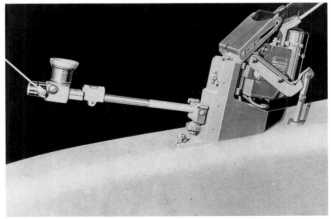

△ A close-up view of the Revi C12D gun-sight still fitted with the sight adjustment instrument.

B-2: Forged in Combat

"... although none of these modifications was radical, but rather details, they resulted in a change to a new sub-type, the Hs 129 B-2. This was to be the main Hs 129 sub-type."

With the series production well under way, the Henschel design team, led by *Dipl.-Ing.* Nicolaus, continued to work on improving its brainchild. By May 1942, it had formulated a number of minor modifications, aimed at improving the weakness of the design, which had emerged as a result of flight trials and the introduction in operational service of the first Hs 129 B-1s on the Eastern Front. These improvements included modifying the engine cowlings to improve cooling and replacing the small diameter circular engine air intakes with larger surface of a rectangular shape, which also incorporated superior sand/dust filters. The fuel system was also modified, incorporating a pressure regulator fitted near the fuel filter and engine fuel pump. Feeder pumps installed in the wing fuel tanks reduced the risk of fuel vapour lock under tropical conditions. The wide-base mid-fuselage antenna was replaced with a narrow-based slimmer one, improving the aerodynamics. The landing light mounted on the port wing's leading edge was deleted. Although none of these modifications were radical, but small details, they resulted in a change to a new sub-type, the Hs 129 B-2. This was to be the main Hs 129 variant, representing over 90 per cent of the total Hs 129 production run. Immediately upon approval, the modifications were incorporated into the airframes under construction, which were the last ten B-1 units (W.Nr. 0201-0210), which were thus renamed B-2s. The first B-2 (W.Nr. 0201) rolled out in mid-May 1942. Later on, further minor modifications were implemented while production was under way which did not result in a sub-type modification, however (including shortened exhaust pipes, deletion of the mid-fuselage antenna mast and the entry-step lock release tiller, and an additional air inlet orifice in the nose section).

With increasing focus being given to the manufacture of the matured B-2 (although still waiting for a new, more powerful engine to become available), the pace of production increased tenfold, from three B-1s in January 1942 to 31 aircraft in April. The 80th series production Hs 129 B (50 B-1 + 30 B-2) was completed on 30 June. At this point, the RLM ordered 928 new units, bringing up the total to 1,008 aircraft, which were to be delivered by December 1944. On 30 September, the 146th Hs 129 B was completed. At that date, according to *Lieferplan* 222, the RLM further increased the overall total to 1,128 aircraft, based on the completion of 40 aircraft per month. The final delivery date was set for 30 March 1945. However, the RLM expressly specified that a new powerplant was to be fitted into any further series production airframe. No detail was given as to the new engine type, possibly because the uncertainty in availability of other, higher performance German engines, badly needed for other important aircraft programmes.

Constant RLM demands for improvements, combined with contradictory orders – such as the requirement asking for *Schleppkupplung* (towing coupling) to be installed on the modified tail cone, (for the planned towing of DFS 230 assault gliders) of six aircraft (W.Nr. 0351-0356, GG+EX and VE+NA to VE+NE) slowed production down considerably, the monthly average barely raising above 20 units – half the planned rate. The first significant increase in production was attained in October 1942, when 33 aircraft were completed at Johannisthal. Monthly production output reached the planned 40 aircraft only in June 1943. Production remained steady until December, when the first Allied bombings directly affecting Henschel *Flugzeugwerk* occurred. It would never reach the 40 aircraft per month rate again, due to the continuous Allied raids, shortage of raw materials and lack of skilled manpower, combined with contradictory orders from the RLM.

In addition to confusing demands, the Henschel *Flugzeugwerk* also became involved, to an increasing extent, in the sub-contracted manufacture of other aircraft types as well. For example, the more complex Junkers Ju 88 A bomber was also being built there in the autumn of 1942, in numbers exceeding that of the Hs 129. Soon the RLM instructed Henschel *Flugzeugwerk* to convert to the manufacture of the more advanced Ju 188. In March 1943, when the necessary tools, jigs and production plans were almost 100 per cent completed, a new RLM order scrapped everything and notified Henschel to retool to mass-produce the Messerschmitt Me 410 twin-engine 'fast' bomber and reconnaissance aircraft, at an astounding rate of 400 aircraft per month. In December 1943, after performing over 400,000 man-hours for the new project, yet another instruction arrived from the RLM, cancelling the previous order and changing the planned production to the Ju 388. Due to this confusing and constantly changing situation, and a great deal of wasted time and effort, the total output at Henschel *Flugzeugwerk* in 1943 was only 61 per cent of their existing production capacity.

An additional factor that contributed to the unsteady production output of the Henschel *Flugzeugwerk* was the increasing lack of sufficient numbers of skilled workers. This issue was partly answered by using foreign workers. At the end of 1939, Henschel's work force was 100 per cent German, but a year later, 3.2 per cent were French prisoners of war. By December 1943, the percentage of foreign workers increased to almost 35 per cent: 16.3 per cent Russian and Ukrainian, 8.2 per cent Polish, 5.8 per cent French, 2.9 per cent Italian and 1.6 per cent other. This employment of foreign workers resulted not only in decreased productivity, but also increased the possibility of sabotage. Besides the human factor, the increasing lack of raw materials and semi-finished products adversely affected the rate of production as well. All these factors contributed to a general decrease in the number and quality of aircraft delivered.

On 30 November 1942, the *Generalluftzeugmeister*, Erhard Milch, in charge of overall aircraft production, instructed all German aircraft companies to change the system of tracking their aircraft's construction numbers from using four or five-digit to a six-digit number, to be issued in intermittent blocks so to confuse enemy espionage. Henschel complied. Accordingly, the new batch of 400 B-2s were tentatively

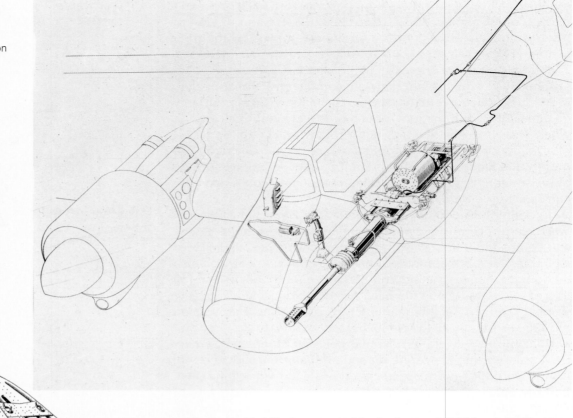

▷ An RLM handbook drawing showing the installation of the 30 mm MK 101 cannon under the fuselage.

△ **Handbook drawing of the rear fuselage showing the tail-plane attachment points**
1 – Hole for rear jacking point
2 – Upper connection points for towing frame
3 – Lower connection points for towing frame
4 – Cable linkage point

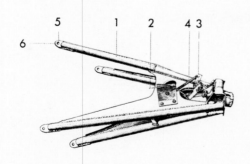

△ **Detail of removable towing frame**
1 – Towing frame
2 – Cable release
3 – Coupling
4 and 5 – Bolts
6 – Fuselage connection point

assigned with *Werknummer* blocks in the 140000 range. Further hundreds of aircraft were also ordered for the future and assigned *Werknummern* in the 141000 and 142000 series, with random gaps of tens and multiples left between production batches due to increased security measures. The *Stammkennzeichen* blocks, issued to every newly manufactured aircraft, followed the same logic.

A *Lieferplan* issued by the RLM's GL/C–B 2 II on 25 May 1943, assessing the situation as on 1 April 1943, called for a total of 1,635 Hs 129 B/Cs already built, or to be built, with the following four *Rüstsatz* possibilities – complementary to the standard equipment (again, no numeric designations are given):

1 x 30 mm MK 101 cannon, total 275 aircraft: 153 built by 30 March 1943, 122 pending, to be manufactured by August 1943, with a maximum output of 25 units/month.

Schleppkupplung (Towing Coupling), total 595 aircraft: 101 built by 30 March 1943, 494 pending, to be manufactured by June 1944, with a maximum output of 40 units/month;

1 x 30 mm MK 103 cannon, total 155 aircraft: none built by 30 March 1943, 155 pending, to be manufactured from September 1943 to June 1944, with a maximum output of 30 units/month.

4 x 50 kg ETC bombs or 1 x 500 kg ETC bomb, total 610 aircraft: 292 built by 30 March 1943, 272 pending, to be manufactured by June 1944, with a maximum output of 30 units/month.

◁ A close-up of the starboard side of the aircraft showing the 30 mm MK 101 hanging in its maintenance position to allow access to the ammunition feed drum. Note the panelling covering the MG 151 has been removed to allow compete access to the gun and its installation.

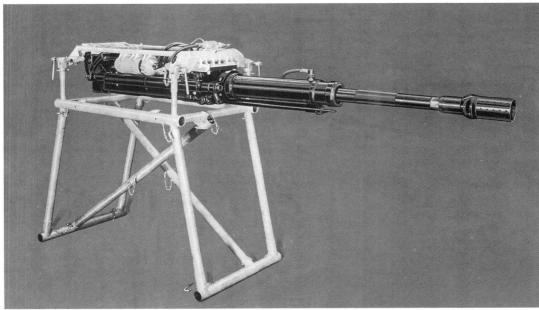

△ Front view of the MK 101 on an Hs 129 B-1 after completion of servicing the gun.

◁ An MK 101 30 mm cannon on its maintenance stand.

▽ Two armourers fix an MK 101 cannon into position with the help of removable lever arms.

◁ A close-up of the MK 101 cannon, complete with shell drum. The oval sheet metal cover is not present to allow a better view of the weapon. The tubular steel frame under the MK 101 was used to hold the weapon for maintenance or display purposes.

△ One of the first Hs 129 B-1s to be fitted with the 30 mm MK 101 underbelly cannon. The gondola containing the gun is hinged to port to allow quick servicing of the main weapon, and is seen in the open position. The drum containing the armour piercing shells has not yet been installed.

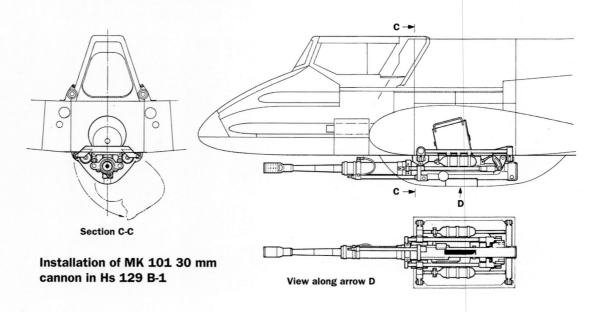

Section C-C

Installation of MK 101 30 mm cannon in Hs 129 B-1

View along arrow D

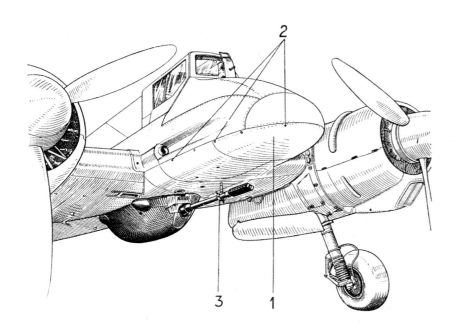

◁ **Handbook drawing of the 30 mm MK 103 cannon as installed in an Hs 129 B-1 and B-2:**
1 – Metal panelling
2 – Countersunk fixing screws
3 – Gun barrel support and adjustment eye

▽ Installation of an MK 103 cannon in the Hs 129 B-2.

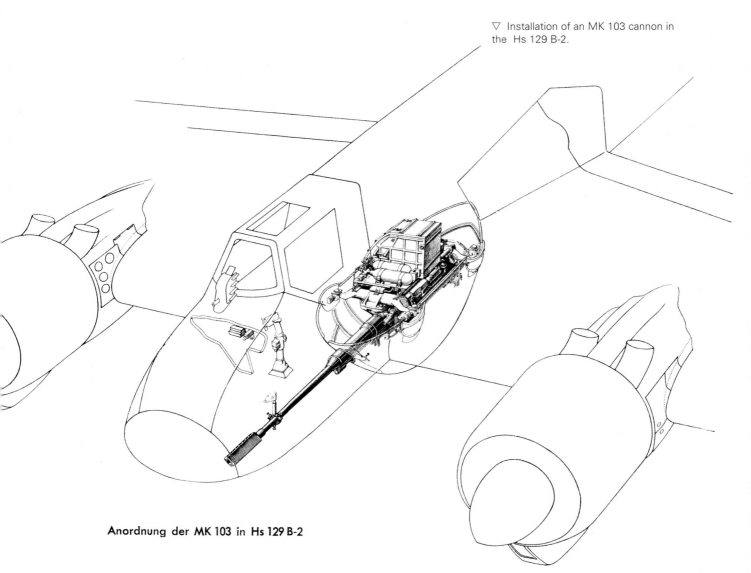

Anordnung der MK 103 in Hs 129 B-2

▷ An Oberfeldwebel closes the collars securing the barrel of the highly effective MK 103 cannon, prior to a combat sortie. The collar ensured that the barrel would not vibrate while the aircraft was in flight. The dark smudge over the muzzle is burnt powder from the cannon blasts. The shallow hollow in the lower nose section, just above the muzzle incorporated a blast panel, which protected the metal skin of the aircraft from the exhaust blast.

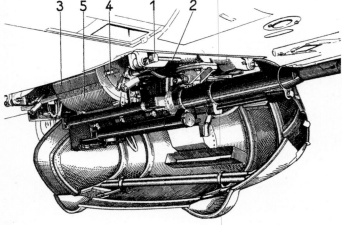

△ **RLM drawing showing the cover to the MK 103, released on its hinges to allow access to the gun for maintenance and re-arming:**
1 – Main hinge bolts
2 – MK 103 ammunition drum swung into access position
3 – Ammunition feed collar
4 – Release catch
5 – Metal cover

▽ **RLM drawing showing the MK 103 in the down position with fairing removed:**
1 – Main bearers with slip bolts
2 – Ammunition drum
3 – Quick release latches for access to drum

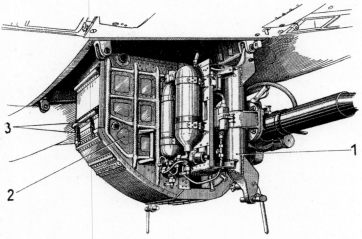

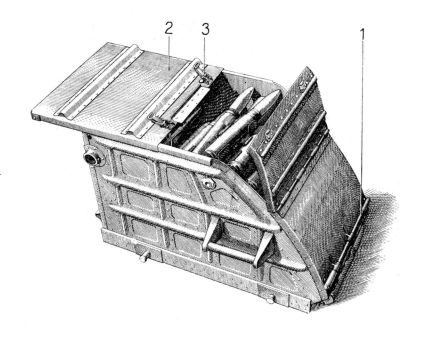

◁ **Factory drawing showing a fully loaded MK 103 ammunition box:**
1 – Closing strap
2 – Lid
3 – Quick release catch

▽ **Weapon instruments in cockpit:**
1 – Security switch
2 – Weapon selection lever
3 – Firing button
4 – Locking control lamp

△ Armourers work to re-load the magazine on a Hs 129 B-2 with 30 mm armour piercing shells. Note that the cover of the MK 103 has been removed in order to gain free access to the gun.

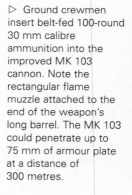

▷ Ground crewmen insert belt-fed 100-round 30 mm calibre ammunition into the improved MK 103 cannon. Note the rectangular flame muzzle attached to the end of the weapon's long barrel. The MK 103 could penetrate up to 75 mm of armour plate at a distance of 300 metres.

Due sometimes to confusing orders, as well as frequent changes in short and long-term plans, production output was unsteady. RLM reports mention only 248 Hs 129 Bs delivered by the end of 1942. The production output figure increased to 331 by March 1943; however, losses had increased dramatically as well. By the same month, an impressive 212 aircraft, i.e., over 64 per cent, were already lost! By September 1943, BAL (*Bauaufsicht des Reichsluftfahrt-ministerium*, abbreviated as *Bauaufsicht Luft*, approximately 'Air Construction Supervision', in charge of accepting newly manufactured aircraft on behalf of the RLM) had accepted 560 aircraft, by which time an even higher percentage, 68 per cent, or 383 aircraft, had already been destroyed in combat, accidents, or abandoned in Africa or Russia. By the end of 1943, the total number of accepted Hs 129 Bs rose to 664, with 495 mentioned as *zerstört* (destroyed) – an extraordinary 75 per cent loss rate! (It is not clear, however, if these statistics refer only to aircraft in *Luftwaffe* service, or also include the exports and the aircraft loaned to the Rumanians). From the spring of 1943, production was constantly plagued by unpredictable demands formulated by the RLM. Losses caused

△ Hs 129 B-2, 'White O', in service with 10.(Pz.)/SG 9, reportedly photographed at Czernowitz (Chernovtsy, Cernauti), in Rumanian administered Bukovina, in the spring of 1944. The gun troughs are blackened, brought about by carbon deposits as a result of firing the weapon.

△ Another Hs 129 B-2 of 10.(Pz.)/SG 9, 'White K' is made ready for action.

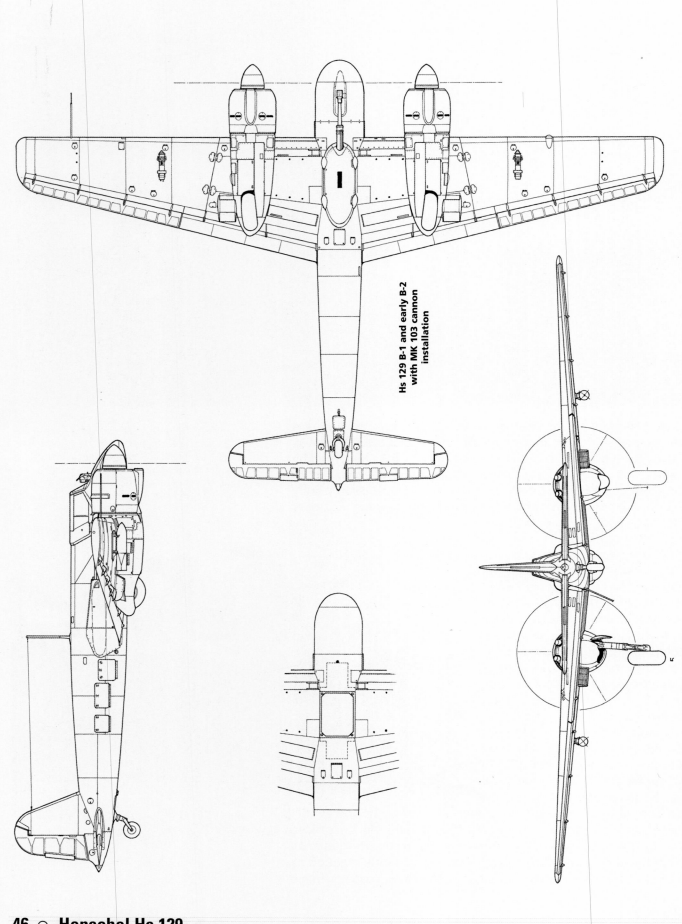

Hs 129 B-1 and early B-2
with MK 103 cannon
installation

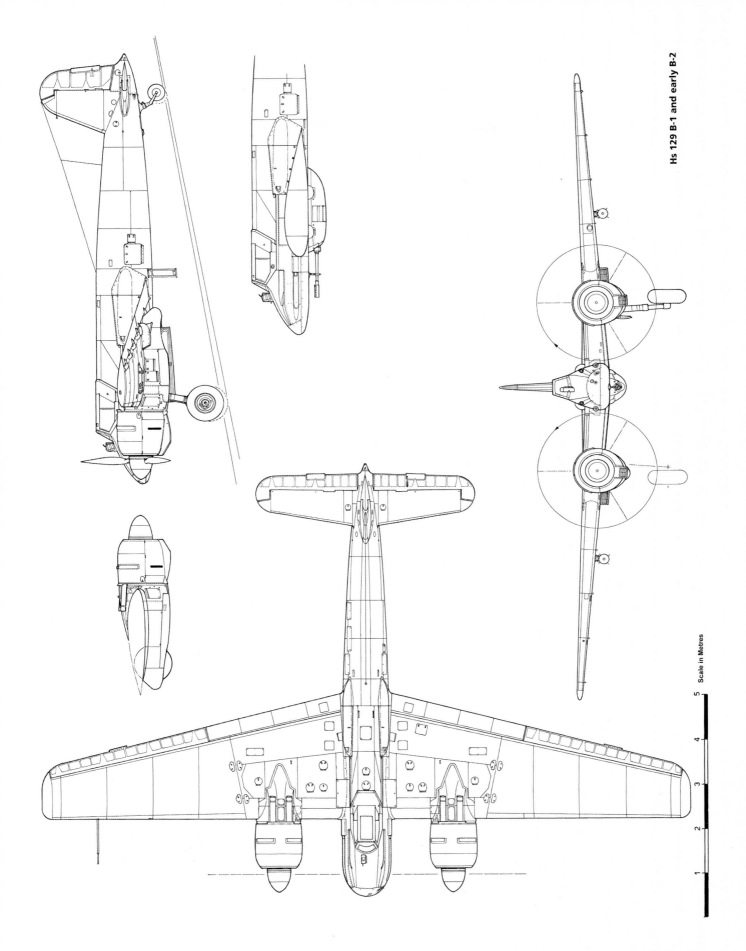

Hs 129 B-1 and early B-2

Scale in Metres

by the increasing number of Allied bombing raids added to the problem (for example, only between late 1943 and early 1944, 34 finished Hs 129 Bs were destroyed by US bombs, which thus were not included in the overall production figure although they were certainly issued *Werknummern*). Bomb damage to various sub-contractors also adversely affected the assembly production. The 414 Hs 129s officially received in 1943 therefore represented less than half the number planned for that year.

The situation did not improve much in 1944. A further setback were the bombing raids that not only disrupted actual production at Henschel, but also seriously affected components supplied by other, smaller factories and workshops. Three Allied bombing raids affected directly the Henschel Works, all in January 1944 (on the 2nd, the 24th and the 29th of the month). Although only three airframes were completely destroyed by the bombs, a further 35 airframes were seriously damaged, most beyond repair. The time needed to repair those that could be salvaged, as well as cleaning up the rubble and restarting production led to further delays.

The last available production data sheet is from 31 March 1944. By then, only 754 Hs 129 Bs were registered as officially delivered, with 510 aircraft (68 per cent) being already written off to various causes, with 244 planned to be built (*im Bestand*) in the near future.

Official Hs 129 B acceptance figures for 1944

Month	Sub-type	Number Accepted	Total planned	Total actual
January	Hs 129 B-2	30	640	614
February	Hs 129 B-2	25	680	639
March	Hs 129 B-2	35	720	674
April	Hs 129 B-2	35	758	709
	Hs 129 C-1	0	2	0
May	Hs 129 B-2	35	792	744
	Hs 129 C-1	0	8	0
June	Hs 129 B-2	27	No total figures given	
July	Hs 129 B-2	17	No total figures given	
	Hs 129 B-3	1		
August	Hs 129 B-2	0	No total figures given	
	Hs 129 B-3	3		
September	Hs 129 B-2	4	No total figures given	
	Hs 129 B-3	16	Last month reporting Hs 129 acceptance[*]	

These figures represent the official number of aircraft *accepted* monthly by the BAL at HFW Johannisthal.

Actual aircraft *production* was certainly higher. For example, aircraft retained by HFW for test purposes or scrapped are not included in the list.

* Production halted in August.

Not all officially accepted Hs 129 Bs were delivered to the *Luftwaffe*, however. On 12 July 1943, *Luftflotte 4* requested 15 Hs 129 Bs to equip a proposed Hungarian ground attack squadron. Two days later, *Generalstab 6. Abteilung* (Department 6 of the *Luftwaffe's* General Staff) reported that the request could not be fulfilled due to aircraft unavailability. This is rather peculiar in view of the fact that by that time the Rumanians had already received a large batch of Hs 129s to equip their own three-squadron strong assault group already deployed on the Eastern Front. Eventually, four Hs 129 B-2s were handed over to the Hungarians for trials in August 1943, with the aim of forming a ground-attack squadron. However, the test flights were soon halted after one of the Henschels crashed during simulated low-level attacks at Rakamaz gunnery range, killing the Hungarian pilot, 2nd Lt. Henrik Fülöp. Other potential customers enquired as well, namely Spain, Japan and Bulgaria, but no formal purchase was forthcoming. A Spanish order, calling for three Hs 129 Bs, was placed in July 1944; however, no actual deliveries took place. Japan had also requested two Hs 129s in September 1943, but no delivery took place due to the lack of transportation. Similarly, Bulgaria initially considered purchasing the type, but eventually opted for the Ju 87 D Stuka instead.

At the end, the sole foreign customer for Henschel's ground attack aircraft remained *Aeronautica Regala Româna* (The Royal Rumanian Air Force – ARR), which received the first Hs 129 B-2s in May 1943. The number of aircraft handed over to them for front line use rose only to 39 by September. By the end of that month, the Rumanians reported 20 Hs 129s already lost in combat and accidents. All lost or seriously damaged aircraft were continuously replaced by the *Luftwaffe*. Deliveries to the ARR were kept steady right up until Rumania unilaterally switched sides on 23 August 1944, leaving the Axis camp and joining the Allies. By then, over 250 Hs 129 Bs were sold, either for home use and training, or loaned by the *Luftwaffe* for front line use only; 35 aircraft were handed over initially, at the time *Grupul 8 asalt* – the 8th Assault Group, the ARR's specialized ground-attack unit – was formed in mid-1943. Later on, during 14 months of combat operations, 122 new and 84 repaired aircraft were gradually handed over to the Rumanians to replace losses. Out of this total number, 43 were lost and 166 damaged, which were then returned to the Germans. The 32 Hs 129 B-2s still existing with *Grupul 8 asalt* on 23 August 1944, at the time of the royal coup, were 'kept' by the Rumanians and used in combat against their former owners. Additionally to these numbers, 15 aircraft were ordered on 28 January 1944, delivered by Henschel directly to Rumania between June and August 1944. It has to be mentioned that the Rumanians used their Hs 129s purely as bombers and none had the 30 mm underbelly cannon installed. This practice continued after the 23 August 1944 about-face, when the Henschel *Schlachtflugzeuge* were employed by the Rumanians against their former allies for nine months, up until the end of the war.

▽ The cover of a 1944 RLM handbook for the B-1 and B-2 variants of the Hs 129, of which some pages have been reproduced over the following pages and elsewhere in this book.

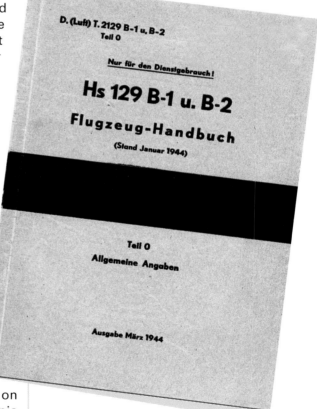

D. (Luft) T. 2129 B-1 u. B-2
Teil 0

Nur für den Dienstgebrauch!

Hs 129 B-1 u. B-2

Flugzeug-Handbuch

(Stand Januar 1944)

Teil 0

Allgemeine Angaben

Ausgabe März 1944

Flugzeugübersicht

Nr.	Benennung	Einbauort
1	Lufterhitzer (ab W. Nr. 0331)	RVT, Stirnwand der P-Kabine
2	Boschhorn (bis W. Nr. 0300)	RVT, Führerraum
3	Seitensteuerpedal mit Bremsfußpumpe	RVT, Führerraum
4	Hauptschalttafel	RVT, unter der P-Kabine
5	Handgriff für Bombennotzug	RVT, Führergerätetafel
6	Revi	RVT, oben
7	Steuerknüppel für Höhen- und Quer-steuerung	RVT, Führerraum
8	Waffenschalttafel	RVT, unter der P-Kabine
9	Führersitz	RVT, Führerraum
10	Führersitzverstellung	RVT, Führerraum
11	Drucköbehälter für Druckölanlage	RMT, zwischen Spant 1 und 2
12	Zerstörkörper	RMT, linke Rumpfseitenwand
13	MG 17	RMT, links und rechts
14	Kraftstoffbehälter 200 l	RMT, zwischen Spant 1 und 3
15	Preßluftflasche für MG 17	RMT, MG 17 links und rechts
16	Arbeitszylinder für Landeklappe	RMT, Spant 3
17	Schalttafel RMT	RMT, Spant 3
18	Leergurtkasten für MG 151	RMT, Rumpfboden zwischen Spant 3 u. 4
19	Akku	RMT, Rumpfdecke zwischen Spant 3 u. 4
20	MG 151	RMT, links und rechts
21	Edukasten für MG 151	RMT, vor Spant 4 links und rechts
23	Gerät FuG 16 z	RHT, zwischen Spant 3 und 4
24	ZBK 24l/1	RHT, Rumpfboden vor Spant 4
25	Sanitätskasten	RHT, linke Rumpfseitenwand
26	Kofferraum	RHT, rechts
27	Mutterkompaß	RHT, Spant 6
28	Antenne FuG 16 z	Außenbord RHT-Seitenflosse
29	Elektrische Trimmruderverstellgetriebe	Höhenruder- und Seitenrudernase
30	Hecklicht	Rumpfende
31	Kraftstoffbehälter 2×205 l	TMT, zwischen Querwand 1 a und 2, links und rechts
32	Vollgurtkasten für MG 17	TMT, Vorderholm
33	Vollgurtkasten für MG 151	TMT, Hinterholm
34	Handgriff: Notzug für Kühlerklappen	RVT, rechte Handhebelbrücke
35	Hebel für Landeklappenbetätigung	RVT, rechte Handhebelbrücke
36	Hebel für Fahrwerkbetätigung	RVT, rechte Handhebelbrücke
37	Sitzkissenfallschirm	RVT, Führersitz
38	Hebel für Brandhahnbetätigung	RVT, linke Handhebelbrücke
39	Gashebel	RVT, linke Handhebelbrücke
40	Gemischhebel	RVT, linke Handhebelbrücke
41	Hebel für 110%-Leistung	RVT, linke Handhebelbrücke
42	Bereitschaftsbüchse (Gasmaske)	TMT, links
43	Motorbrandlöscher	Fahrwerkskabine
44	SS-Arbeitszylinder für Fahrwerk	Fahrwerkskabine
45	Schmierstoffbehälter 2×35 l	TMT, zwischen Querwand 3 und 4, links und rechts
46	Scheinwerfer	linke Tragfläche
47	Robot	rechte Tragfläche
48	Staurohr	rechte Tragfläche
49	Flugzeugkennlicht (links rot, rechts grün)	linke und rechte Tragfläche

△▽ Equipment layout.

C. Aufbau des Flugzeugbaumusters

Flugzeugübersicht

50 ○ **Henschel Hs 129**

Nr.	Aufschrift	Schriftart
1	Haube öffnen! Nach Öffnen der Scheibe Hebel an der linken Kabinenseite ziehen!	Fette Mittelschrift 10 DIN 1451 rot
2	△ Druckölanlage „Fl-Drucköl"	Fette Mittelschrift 10 DIN 1451 rot
3	△ Kraftstoff-Kennzeichnung B 4	LgN 16 616
4	Akku	Fette Mittelschrift 16 DIN 1451 rot
5	Drücken für Leiter (nur bis W. Nr. 0290)	HsN 16 625.37
6	Handgriffklappe	HsN 16 625.36
7	Bordsack	Fette Mittelschrift 10 DIN 1451 weiß
8	Hier anheben	HsN 16 625.10
9	Einstellehre	HsN 16 625.45
10	Nicht anfassen	HsN 16 625.7
11	Kennzeichnung für Feststellscheren	Siehe Punkt A
12	Kennzeichnung für Höhenflossen-einstellung	Siehe Nivelliermeßblatt, Abb. 17
13	Reifendruck 3,5 atü	HsN 16 625.13
14	Verankerung	HsN 16 625.6
15	Hier Lagerjoch	HsN 16 625.11
16	Pfeil	HsN 16 625.2
17	Motorbezüge (Kofferraum RHT)	Fette Mittelschrift 12,5 DIN 1451 weiß
18	Preßluft	HsN 16 625.8
19	Rotes Kreuz	HsN 16 625.27
20	Handkurbel mit Verlängerung	Fette Mittelschrift 10 DIN 1451 weiß
21	Bordbuch, Schematasche	Fette Mittelschrift 10 DIN 1451 weiß
22	Werkzeugtasche	Fette Mittelschrift 10 DIN 1451 rot
23	Bezug für Laufrad	Fette Mittelschrift 10 DIN 1451 rot
24	Zerstörkörper	Fette Mittelschrift 10 DIN 1451 rot
25	Für Bremsen „Fl-D"	Fette Mittelschrift 10 DIN 1451 schwarz
26	Reifendruck 4 atü	Fette Mittelschrift 10 DIN 1451 schwarz
27	Hier aufbocken	HsN 16 625.5
28	Kennzeichnung für Landeklappen-einstellung	Siehe Zeichnung 129.502/512 Bl. 4
29	△ Schmierstoff-Kennzeichnung Aero Shell mittel	HsN 16 625.51
30	Hier aufheißen	HsN 16 625.17
31	Nur hier betreten	HsN 16 625.33
32	Siehe Text auf der Abbildung (bis W. Nr. 0188)	Fette Mittelschrift 8 DIN 1451 weiß
33	Bereitschaftsbüchse (Gasmaske) MP und Stahlhelm	Fette Mittelschrift 10 DIN 1451 weiß
34	Füllmarke für Stoßdämpfer (roter Strich)	Fette Mittelschrift 10 DIN 1451 schwarz
35	Preßluftanschluß für Druckspeicher (ab W. Nr. 0331)	Fette Mittelschrift 10 DIN 1451 weiß
36	Außenbordanschluß für Druckölanlage (ab W. Nr. 0331)	Fette Mittelschrift 16 DIN 1451 schwarz
37	Ziehen für Leiter (ab W. Nr. 0291)	Fette Mittelschrift 16 DIN 1451 weiß
38	Luftfilter nach jedem zweiten Start reinigen	Fette Mittelschrift 10 DIN 1451 schwarz
	Bei Winterbetrieb wegen Vereisungsgefahr mit offener Nebeneinlaßklappe fliegen	
39	Endkappe für Re (ab W. Nr. 0331)	Fette Mittelschrift 10 DIN 1451 weiß

△▽ Writing and stencilling.

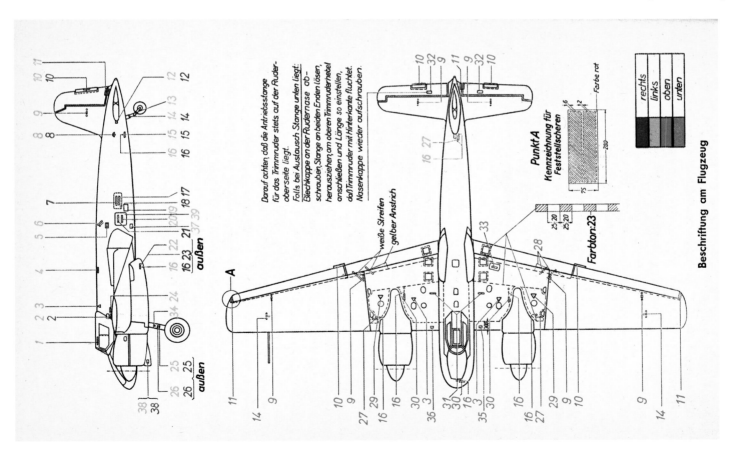

Darauf achten, daß die Antriebsstange für das Trimmruder stets auf der Ruder-oberseite liegt.
Falls bei Austausch Stange unten liegt: Blechkappe an der Rudernase ab-schrauben, Stange an beiden Enden lösen, herausziehen, am oberen Trimmruderhebel anschließen und Länge so einstellen, daß Trimmruder mit Hinterkante fluchtet. Nasenkappe wieder aufschrauben.

weiße Streifen
gelber Anstrich

Punkt A
Kennzeichnung für Feststellscheren

Farbton: 23

Farbe rot

rechts
links
oben
unten

Beschriftung am Flugzeug

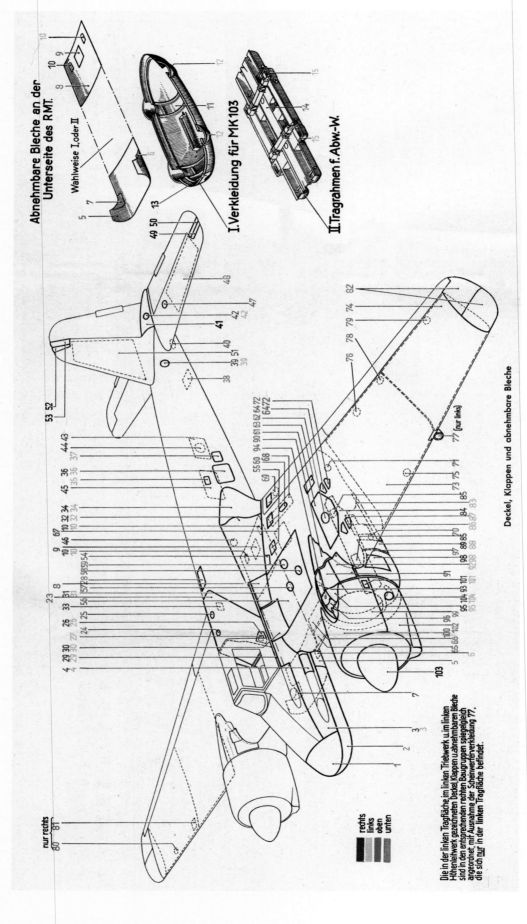

Abnehmbare Bleche an der
Unterseite des RMT.

Wahlweise I. oder II

I. Verkleidung für MK 103

II. Tragrahmen f. Abw.-w.

Deckel, Klappen und abnehmbare Bleche

Die in der linken Tragfläche, im linken Triebwerk u. im linken
Höhenleitwerk gezeichneten Deckel, Klappen u. abnehmbaren Bleche
sind in den entsprechenden rechten Baugruppen spiegelgleich
angeordnet, mit Ausnahme der Scheinwerferverkleidung 77,
die sich nur in der linken Tragfläche befindet.

rechts
links
oben
unten

△ Covers, flaps and removable panels.
Code colours: Blue = right (starboard side)
Yellow = left (port side)
Red = upper (uppersurfaces)
Green = lower (undersurfaces)

Deckel, Klappen und abnehmbare Bleche

(Siehe Abb. 10 und Seite 21 bis 24)

Nr.	Lage	Zweck	Befestigung durch
1	Rumpfvorderteil, vorn	Zugang zur vorderen Wand der Panzerkabine, Heißbeschlag, Heizaggregat	Schnellverschlüsse
2	Rumpfvorderteil, unten	Zugang zu den Befestigungsbolzen für Panzerplatte, zu den elektrischen Schalttafeln und den unteren Trennstellen zwischen RVT und RMT	Schnellverschluß
3	Rumpfvorderteil, links und rechts	Übergangsverkleidung: Zugang zu den Trennstellen zwischen RVT und RMT, zur Handpumpe und zum Umschalter für Drucköl anlage, Fertigung und Zusammenbau	Schnellverschluß
4	Rumpfvorderteil, links und rechts	Seitenjustierung des MG 17	Linsensenkschrauben
5	Rumpfmittelteil, unten	Zugang zur unteren Aufhängung der Panzerkabine und zu den unteren Trennstellen zwischen RVT und RMT; Höhenjustierung für MG 17	Schnellverschlüsse
6	Rumpfmittelteil, unten links	Zugang zum Preßluftanschluß für Druckspeicher der Drucköl anlage, Elt-Leitungen	Schnellverschlüsse
7	Rumpfmittelteil, unten rechts	Zugang zu Drucköl anlage, Elt-Leitungen	Schnellverschlüsse
8	Rumpfmittelteil, unten	Zugang zu den Einbauten im RMT	Flügelmuttern
9	Rumpfmittelteil, unten Mitte	Entleeren des Hülsenkastens	Schnellverschlüsse
10	Rumpfmittelteil, unten links und rechts	links: Blinddeckel; rechts: Zugang zum Anschluß des Zünderbatteriekastens ZBK 241/1	Schnellverschlüsse
11	Rumpfmittelteil, unten	Verkleidung für MK 103	Linsenschrauben
12	Rumpfmittelteil, unten links	} I Zugang zu den Verbindungsbolzen für Anschluß der MK 103 an den Rumpf	Scharnier
13	Rumpfmittelteil, unten	} II Anbaugründe	Verriegelung
14	Rumpfmittelteil, unten	Verkleidung für Tragrahmen der Abwurfwaffe	Verriegelung
15	Rumpfmittelteil, unten links	Zugang zu den Anschlußstellen für Tragrahmen der Abwurfwaffe	Linsensenkschrauben
23	Rumpfmittelteil, oben	Kraftstoffbehälteraus- und -einbau	Linsensenkschrauben
24	Rumpfmittelteil, oben	Zugang zum Füllkopf für den Kraftstoffbehälter	Schnellverschlüsse
25	Rumpfmittelteil, oben	Zugang zum Kraftstoffbehälterkopf (Anschluß der Leitungen)	Schnellverschluß
26	Rumpfmittelteil, links und rechts	Zugang zum Auffüllen der Drucköl behälter	Schnellverschluß
27	Rumpfmittelteil, links	Zugang zum Zerstörkörper	Scheibe
28	Rumpfmittelteil, oben	Zugang zur Batterie für Elt-Ausrüstung	Schnellverschlüsse
29	Rumpfmittelteil, links und rechts	Zugang zu den Haubenführungen	Linsensenkschrauben

Nr.	Lage	Zweck	Befestigung durch
30	Rumpfmittelteil, links und rechts	Wartung des MG 17	Schnellverschluß
31	Rumpfmittelteil, links und rechts	Wartung des MG 17	Schnellverschluß
32	Rumpfmittelteil, links und rechts	Wartung des MG 151	Schnellverschlüsse
33	Rumpfmittelteil, rechts	Zugang zur elektr. Schalttafel am Spant 3, RMT	Schnellverschluß
34	Rumpfhinterteil, links und rechts	Ein- und Ausbau des EDSK 151 B für MG 151	Linsensenkschrauben
35	Rumpfhinterteil, links	Handgriff zum Auslösen der Aufstiegleiter	Scharnier mit Federn
36	Rumpfhinterteil, links und rechts	Zugang zum Geräteblock der Funkanlage; rechts: auch ZBK 241/1	Schnellverschlüsse
37	Rumpfhinterteil, links	Zugang zum Sanitätspack	Schnellverschluß
38	Rumpfhinterteil, unten	Zugang zum Umlenkhebel für Höhensteuerung, Ein- und Ausbau des Sporns	Linsensenkschrauben
39	Rumpfhinterteil, links und rechts	Zugang zum Umlenkhebel für Höhensteuerung, Ein- und Ausbau des Sporns	Schnellverschlüsse
40	Rumpfhinterteil, unten	Prüfung der Steuerung im Rumpfhinterteil	Linsensenkschrauben
41	Rumpfhinterteil, Endkappe	Zugang zum Steuerungsgestänge im Rumpfhinterteil, zum unteren Seitenruderlager, zum mittleren Höhenruderlager, Leitwerksmontage	Linsensenkschrauben
42	Rumpfhinterteil, in Endkappe links und rechts	Zugang zum Hecklicht, Steuerungsanschluß am Seitenruder	Schnellverschlüsse
43	Rumpfhinterteil, rechts	Ein- und Ausbau des Mutterkompasses	Linsensenkschrauben
44	Rumpfhinterteil, rechts	Justierung des Mutterkompasses	Schnellverschluß
45	Rumpfhinterteil, rechts	Zugang zum Kofferraum, Preßluftanschluß für MG 17	Schnellverschlüsse
46	Rumpfhinterteil, rechts	Außenbordanschluß für elektrisches Bordnetz	Schnellverschluß
47	Höhenflosse links und rechts, oben und unten	Anbau der Höhenflosse an den Rumpf, Zugang zum Bolzen für Höhenflossenverstellung	Schnellverschlüsse
48	Höhenflosse, Unterseite	Zugang zu den Einbauten der Höhenflosse zwecks Prüfung und Wartung	Linsensenkschrauben
49	Höhenruder, Aerodynam. Ausgleich	Fertigungsgründe	Linsensenkschrauben
50	Höhenruder, Ärodynam. Ausgleich	Einbau der Ausgleichsgewichte	Linsensenkschrauben
51	Seitenflosse, rechts	Zugang zu den Einbauten der Seitenflosse zwecks Prüfung und Wartung	Linsensenkschrauben
52	Seitenflosse, Ärodynam. Ausgleich	Fertigungsgründe	Linsensenkschrauben
53	Seitenruder, Ärodynam. Ausgleich	Einbau des Ausgleichsgewichtes	Linsensenkschrauben
54	Tragflächenmittelteil, links und rechts	Zugang zum Zuführungshals für MG 151	Gehalten durch Klappe 32
55	Tragflächenmittelteil, links und rechts	Auftrittklappen	Druckfedern

Nr.	Lage	Zweck	Befestigung durch
56	Tragflächenmittelteil, links und rechts	Kraftstoffbehälterein- und -ausbau	Linsensenkschrauben
57	Tragflächenmittelteil, links und rechts	Zugang zum elektrischen Vorratsgeber für Kraftstoff	Schnellverschlüsse
58	Tragflächenmittelteil, links und rechts	Zugang zum Füllkopf für den Kraftstoffbehälter	Schnellverschlüsse
59	Tragflächenmittelteil, links und rechts	Zugang zum Kraftstoffbehälterkopf (Anschluß der Leitungen)	Schnellverschlüsse
60	Tragflächenmittelteil, links und rechts	Zugang zur Gasmaske	Schnellverschlüsse
61	Tragflächenmittelteil, links und rechts	Schmierstoffbehälterein- und -ausbau	Linsensenkschrauben
62	Tragflächenmittelteil, links und rechts	Zugang zum Füllkopf für den Schmierstoffbehälter	Schnellverschlüsse
63	Tragflächenmittelteil, links und rechts	Zugang zur Aufhängung des Schmierstoffkühlers und zu den Trennstellen der Kühlerleitungen	Linsensenkschrauben
64	Tragflächenmittelteil, links und rechts	Zugang zu den Verbindungsbolzen zwischen Tragflächenmittel- und -außenteil	Schnellverschlüsse
65	Tragflächenmittelteil, links und rechts	Zugang zum Triebwerksbedienungsgestänge in der Tragflächennase	Schnellverschlüsse
66	Tragflächenmittelteil, links und rechts	Einsetzen und Herausnehmen des Vollgurtkastens für MG 17	Spezialverschluß
67	Tragflächenmittelteil, links und rechts	MG 17 Aus- und Einbau	Linsensenkschrauben
68	Tragflächenmittelteil, links und rechts	Einsetzen und Herausnehmen des Vollgurtkastens für MG 151	Spezialverschluß
69	Tragflächenmittelteil, Landeklappe, links und rechts	Links: Zugänglichkeit der Landeklappe für Einbau der Auftrittklappe 55, rechts: blind	Schnellverschlüsse
70	Tragflächenmittelteil, links und rechts	Zugang für Elt.-Trennstellen, rechts: auch zu den Entwässerungsstutzen für Fahrtmesserleitungen	Schnellverschlüsse
71	Tragflächenmittelteil, links und rechts	Zugang für Elt.-Trennstellen Bombennotzug	Schnellverschlüsse
72	Tragflächenaußenteil, links und rechts	Zugang zu den Verbindungsbolzen zwischen Tragflächenmittel- und -außenteil	Schnellverschlüsse
73	Tragflächenaußenteil, links und rechts	Zugang zu den Einbauten; Fertigungsgründe	Linsensenkschrauben
74	Tragflächenaußenteil, links und rechts		Linsensenkschrauben
75	Tragflächenaußenteil, links und rechts	Zugang zu den Elt.-Verbindungen für Abwurfwaffe	Schnellverschlüsse
76	Tragflächenaußenteil, links und rechts	Zugang zu den Elt.-Verbindungen für Abwurfwaffe	Schnellverschlüsse
77	Tragflächenaußenteil, links	Scheinwerferaus- und -Einbau, Zugang zum Elt.-Anschluß für Scheinwerfer	Linsensenkschrauben
78	Tragflächenaußenteil, links und rechts	Zugang zum Umlenkhebel für Querruder bei Querwand 6	Schnellverschlüsse
79	Tragflächenaußenteil, links und rechts	Rechts: Zugang zu den Schlauchverbindungen zwischen Fahrt- und Höhenmesserleitung; Elt.-Stecker für Staurohr links: blind	Schnellverschlüsse
80	Tragflächenaußenteil, rechts	Zugang zur Fahrt- und Höhenmesserleitung und Luftleitung für Staurohr	Schnellverschluß
81	Tragflächenaußenteil, rechts	Kameraein- und -ausbau	Schnellverschluß
82	Tragflächenaußenteil, links und rechts	Zugang zur Elt.-Ausrüstung in den Tragflächenspitzen; Fertigungsgründe	Linsensenkschrauben
83	Fahrwerkskabine, äußere Klappe	Montage der Einbauten in der Fahrwerkskabine	Linsensenkschrauben
84	Fahrwerkskabine, innere Klappe	Verkleidung des eingezogenen Fahrbeins	Gummiseil und Fahrgestellbein
85	Fahrwerkskabine, innere Klappe	Fertigungsgründe: Zugang zum Scharnieren der inneren Klappe	Linsensenkschrauben
86	Fahrwerkskabine	Zugang zur Anlaßgerätetafel	Schnellverschlüsse
87	Fahrwerkskabine	Zugang zum Schnellablaßventil des Schmierstoffbehälters	Schnellverschlüsse
88	Fahrwerkskabine	Auf- und Abbau des Fahrgestells, Zugang zu den Thermometeranschlüssen der Schmierstoffleitungen, zum Bedienungsgestänge für Einspritzpumpen, Bremsleitungen	Linsensenkschrauben
89	Fahrwerkskabine	Auf- und Abbau des Fahrgestells	Linsensenkschrauben
90	Übergang Motorraum-Tragflächenmittelteil	Zugang zum Elt.-Trennstellengehäuse Übergangsverkleidung	Linsensenkschrauben
91	Motorraum, oben	Triebwerkswechsel, Zugang zu Triebwerksleitungen und -geräten	Schnellverschlüsse
92	Motorraum: linker Motor, linke Seite / Motor, rechte Seite	Prüfung der oberen Triebwerksgerüstanschlüsse, Triebwerkswechsel	Schnellverschlüsse
93	Motorraum: linker Motor, rechte Seite, rechter Motor, linke Seite	Prüfung der oberen Triebwerksgerüstanschlüsse, Triebwerkswechsel	Schnellverschlüsse
94	Motorraum, oben	Zugang zu Triebwerksleitungen und -geräten	Schnellverschlüsse
95	Motorraum, oben	Zugang zu den Triebwerksgeräten, Aus- und Einbau des Stromerzeugers	Linsensenkschrauben
96	Motorraum, oben	Fertigungsgründe, Aus- und Einbau des Stromerzeugers	Linsensenkschrauben
97	Motorraum, unten	Triebwerkswechsel, Zugang zu Triebwerksleitungen und -geräten	Schnellverschlüsse
98	Motorraum, links und rechts	Prüfung der unteren Triebwerksgerüstanschlüsse, Zugang zu Triebwerksleitungen	Schnellverschlüsse
99	Motorraum	Zugang zu Triebwerksgeräten	Linsensenkschrauben
100	Motor, oben	Motorverkleidung	Spannverschlüsse
101	Motor, oben	Zugang zur Sicherung des Spannverschlusses der Motorverkleidung	Linsensenkschrauben
102	Motor, unten	Motorverkleidung	Spannverschlüsse
103	Luftschraube	Zugang zur Luftschraubennabe und zum Verstellgetriebe	Linsensenkschrauben
104	Motor, unten	Zugang zum Schmierstoffsumpf und Zündkerzen	Schnellverschlüsse

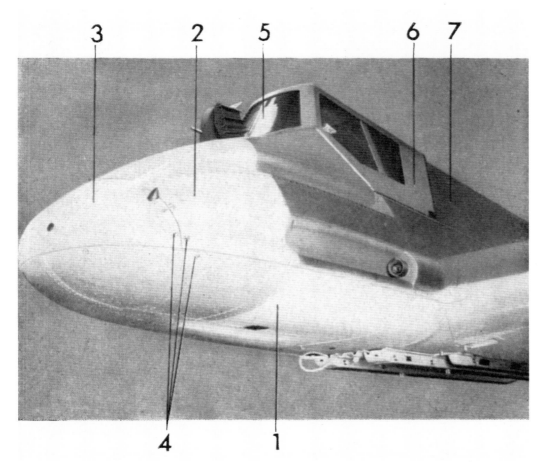

◁ **RLM detail showing the Hs 129 forward fuselage area:**
1 – Underside cover plating
2 – Side covering
3 – Nose covering
4 – Counter-sunk screws
5 – Fixed cockpit windscreen
6 – Sliding canopy
7 – Fuel tank covering

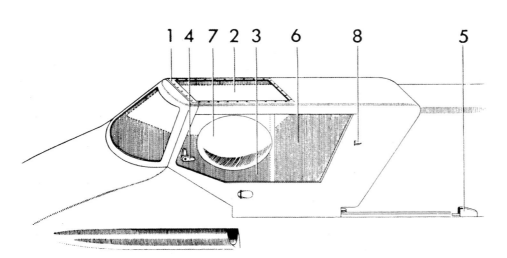

△ **RLM detail of sliding canopy:**
1 – Dural framing
2 – Armour plate glass panel
3 – Sliding glass panel
4 – Sliding panel catch
5 – Stop
6 – Fixed glass panel
7 – Bubble in sliding glass panel
  (Note this does not seem to appear on any Hs 129 aircraft)
8 – Sliding panel stop

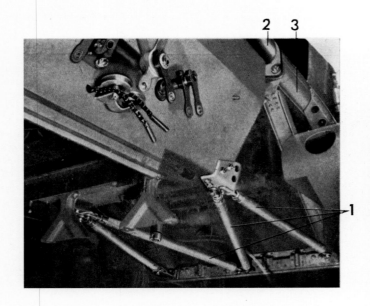

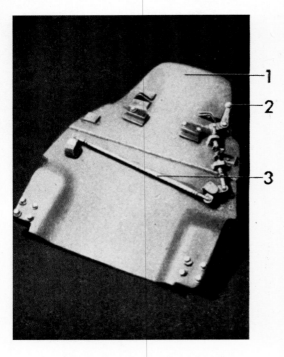

◁ **Attachment points for armoured cockpit:**
1 – Dural structural framing
2 – Gun firing channel in the armoured cockpit
3 – Gun firing channel in the fuselage centre section

△ **Removable armour plate panel behind pilot seat:**
1 – Rear wall
2 – Lever
3 – Locking arm

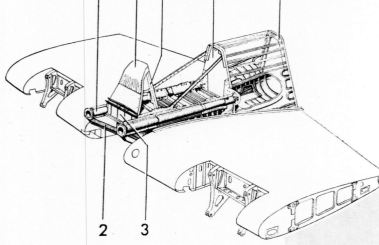

△ **Fuselage centre section:**
1 – Upper spar (gun trough)
2 – Horizontal framing
3 – Fuselage vertical panel
4 – Angled frame
5 – Frame 2
6 – Frame 3
7 – Frame 4

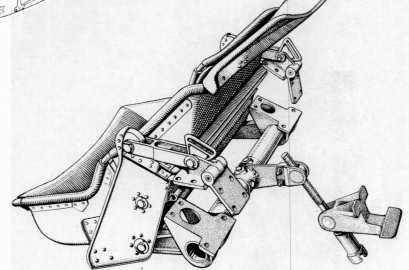

▷ Adjustable armoured pilot's seat and attachment points.

◁ **Fuel tank position behind pilot:**
1 – Position of fuel tank
2 – Tank carrier plates
3 – Fixing straps

◁ **Detail of installed fuel tank and filler cap:**
1 – Fuel tank filler cap
2 – Adjacent filler cap

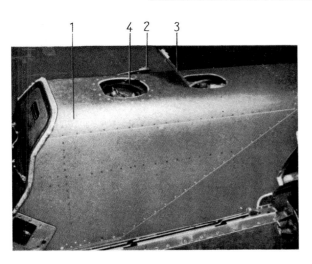

◁ **Detail of fuselage fuel tank covering:**
1 – Covering
2 – Removable cover
3 – Flap
4 – Rubber seal

◁ Port side view of upper fuselage panel showing fixing screws removed with the panel partially moved forward. The fuselage has received flak damage and the panel is being removed for repair. Note the yellow octane triangle with the octane rating B4 painted in black and the emblem of 5./Sch.G 1, the axe wielding Berlin Bear, which was painted black on a blue background. This image has been taken from an RLM handbook devoted to the recovery and repair of the Hs 129.

Berlin Bear badge of 5./Sch.G 1

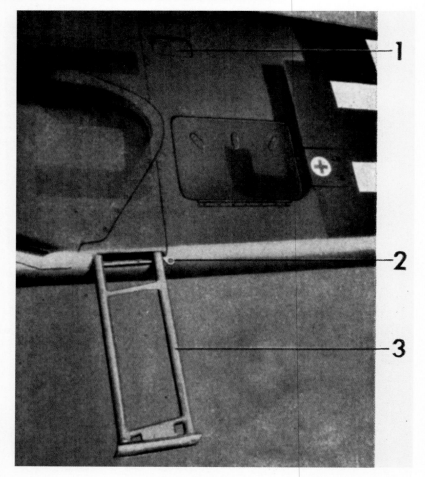

▷ **Retractable entry step:**
1 – Spring loaded hand grip
2 – Latch
3 – Step

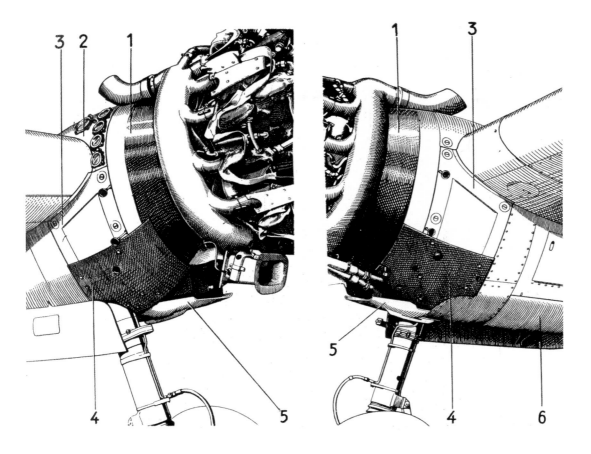

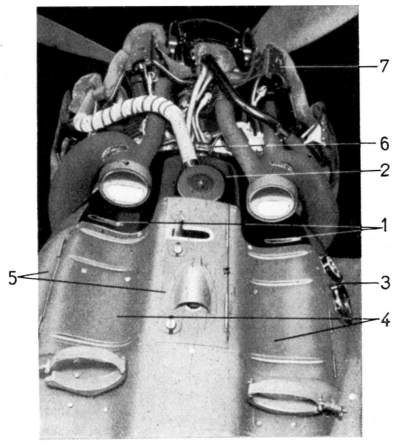

△ **Lower engine covering. Note the short exhaust tubes as fitted to late B-2 variants.**

1 – Front side panel
2 – Instrument panel
3 – Rear side panel
4 – Armour plating
5 – Armour plating to lubricating sump
6 – External lower panelling to undercarriage housing

◁ **Upper engine covering with exhaust tubes removed:**

1 – Exhaust opening
2 – Lid
3 – Instrument panel
4 – Upper part
5 – Flaps
6 – Heat hose
7 – Cowling attachment points

◁ **Fuel filler cap position on the upper wing surface:**
1 – Hand release covers to fuel filler caps
2 – Hand release cover to filler cap for lubricating oil

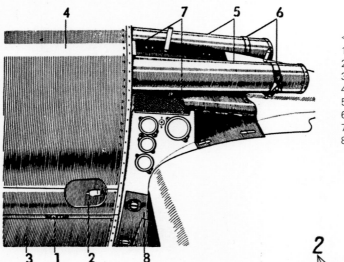

◁ **Engine covering:**
1 – Spring loaded release
2 – Hinged flap
3 – Lower external covering
4 – Top external covering
5 – Exhaust pipes
6 – Fixing clips
7 – Upper part of internal covering
8 – Lower part of internal covering

▷ **Detail of engine mounting:**
1 – Front of engine mounting ring
2 – Tubular struts
3 – Elastic fixing points
4 – Rubber engine mounts

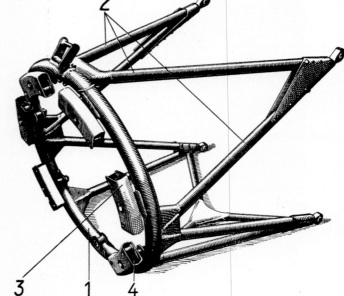

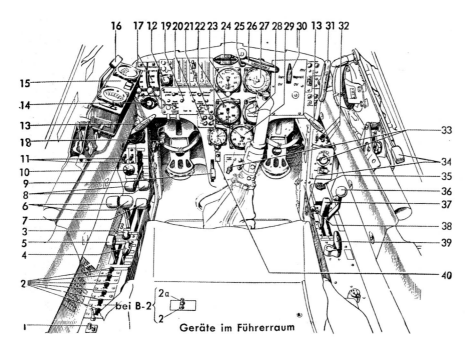

16 17 12 19 20 21 22 23 24 25 26 27 28 29 30 13 31 32

bei B-2 { 2a
          2

Geräte im Führerraum

△ Cockpit instrumentation:

1 – Long-range cut off switch
2 – Switch for camera
      for B-1: fuel tank pump
      for B-2:{2a = wing tank pump
         {2 = fuselage
      Artificial Horizon
      Heating Nozzle
      Position Light
      Landing Lamp
3 – Press Switch for Gun Camera Bay
4 – Mixture Lever
5 – Lever for 110 per cent power (Emergency Boost)
6 – Throttle Levers
7 – Fuel Lever
8 – Fuel Shut-Off Levers (Slow Running)
9 – Cockpit Heating Lever
10 – Undercarriage Selector Switch
11 – Switch for Instrument Lamp, Motor and Cockpit (Cockpit Light)
12 – Dimmer Switch
13 – Fire Extinguisher
14 – Master Cut-Off for Electrics
15 – Switch Box for Rudder Trim Adjustment Indicator
16 – Handle for Cockpit Locking
17 – Magneto Switches
18 – Dimmer Switch for Instrument Lights on the Hand Lever
      Framework
19 – Switch Box for Airscrew Controls
20 – Undercarriage Position Triple Lamp Indicator
21 – Chronometer
22 – Air Speed Indicator
23 – Altimeter
24 – Data Card Holder
25 – Pitot Head Heating Indicator
26 – Cockpit Canopy Emergency Release Lever
27 – Repeater Compass
28 – Artificial Horizon
29 – Twin Manifold Pressure Gauge
30 – SK 244 A (arming selector panel)
31 – Emergency Release for Bomb and External Fuel Tank (B-2)
32 – Heating Transformer Switch for FuG 16 Z

33 – Frequency Switch and Selector for FuG 16 Z
34 – Handle and Viewing Hole for Oil Pressure Hand Pump
      (Undercarriage Emergency Lowering)
35 – Auxiliary Indicator for FuG 16 Z
36 – Landing Flaps Lever
37 – Undercarriage Lever
38 – Safety Switch for Undercarriage Operating Lever
39 – Emergency Operating Handle for Cooling Gills
40 – Control Light for Cockpit Heating

▽ Instrumentation for left motor:

41 – RPM Gauge
42 – Fuel Contents Gauge
43 – Fuel Flow Gauge
44 – Lubricating Oil Temperature Gauge
45 – Fuel and Oil Pressure Gauge
46 – Pressure Gauge for Pressurised Oil System

▽ Instrumentation for right motor:

47 – RPM Gauge
48 – Fuel Contents Gauge
49 – Fuel Flow Gauge
50 – Lubricating Oil Temperature Gauge
51 – Fuel and Oil Pressure Gauge

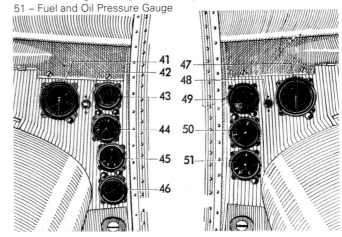

Advanced Weapon and Equipment Trials

"...the latter was fitted with the impressive 3.7 cm BK 3,7 gun - a modified Flak 18 anti-aircraft cannon - with 12 rounds in a gondola placed under the fuselage..."

▽ An early production Hs 129 B-2, W.Nr. 0280 (DQ+ZO), armed with an underbelly Flak 18 cannon. A conical-shaped flash eliminator on the barrel's muzzle shielded the pilot from the bright flash produced when the weapon was fired.

Even in the early stages of series production, when every Hs 129 was badly needed to equip the fledgling *Luftwaffe Schlacht* air units, several aircraft were retained by Henschel for various equipment and weapon trials. As noted earlier, W.Nr. 129 3007, a pre-series A-0, was the first aircraft to be converted to B-0 standards. Another one withheld from delivery was W.Nr. 0016, the first true B-0 series aircraft, assigned to *Temperaturmeßflüge* (temperature – i.e. engine temperature – measurement flights) at the end of 1942. The next aircraft diverted by Henschel were from the initial B-2 batch. *Werknummern* 0266, 0267 and 0280 were withheld in the summer of 1943, the first two for *allgemeine Flugeigenschaften* (General Flight Characteristics) and *allgemeine Flugerprobung* (General Flight Testing), while the latter was fitted with the impressive 3.7 cm BK 3,7 gun – a modified *Flak 18* anti-aircraft cannon – with 12 rounds in a gondola placed under the fuselage. The same weapon was also fitted under each wing of the Junkers Ju 87 G Stuka tank-killer, the preferred weapon of choice of the most efficient and most decorated all-time ground-attack ace, *Oberst* Hans-Ulrich Rudel. The BK 3,7 installation required the removal of the two 7.92 mm MG 17 machine guns from the nose section, in order to reduce weight.

In September 1943, two further B-2s were retained by Henschel for the experimental role: W.Nr. 141253 and 141256, both as flying test beds for various, unspecified types of armament. On the first day of the following month, W.Nr. 140494, DO+XG, was recalled from the Tarnewitz test centre to Henschel Schönefeld, in order to be equipped with the awesome, 7.5 cm calibre BK (*Bordkanone*, on-board cannon). It became the prototype for the new B-3 sub-version. Some

◁ Another view of W.Nr. 0280 (DQ+ZO). This was the first Henschel fitted with the Flak 18 large-calibre weapon in the summer of 1943. Flight trials were carried out at Rechlin and it was found that the weapon caused adverse effects on the aircraft's flying characteristics, especially when landing, and trials were eventually discontinued in October 1943.

△ The same BK 3,7 cannon was also fitted to the 'tank-killer' version of the famous Stuka, the Ju 87 G.

△▽▷ These close-up photographs show Henschel technicians attaching the gondola housing the 3.7cm calibre Rheinmetall Flak 18 cannon fitted under the fuselage of an Hs 129 B. The barrel of this modified anti-aircraft cannon was not yet installed in the upper front opening. After this modified weapon passed its firing tests, it was redesigned BK (Bordkanone) 3,7. This weapon was supplied with 12 rounds of armour piercing ammunition.

Advanced Weapon and Equipment Trials ○ 63

sources identify this sub-type as the Hs 129 B-3/Wa. However, this is a misinterpretation of an official Henschel factory manual's title, where 'Wa' is merely the short form of *Waffen*, or weapon. The same is valid for the spurious Hs 129 B-2/Wa sub-type. Next day, another Hs 129 B-2, W.Nr. 141291, arrived, followed two days later by the next aircraft in the production list, W.Nr. 141292. Both were assigned to trials with a 5 cm cannon

△▽ Hs 129 B-2, W.Nr. 140494 coded DO+XG was one of the first aircraft modified to B-3 standard, carrying the 7.5 cm BK cannon. This machine was flown at the Erprobungsstelle Rechlin test centre in June 1944 to assess control vibrations and flight characteristics. It was fitted with an enlarged rudder and then transferred to the weapons testing centre at Tarnewitz on 8 July 1944.

(BK 5). During October, tests with the 3.7 cm *Flak* 18 were halted because the aircraft's flying and landing characteristics had suffered severely. In lieu, tests with the astounding 7.5 cm BK 7,5 commenced. Also in October, at the suggestion of the *Führer des Panzerjäger* (Commander of Anti-Tank Units), *Hauptmann* Eggers, tests were undertaken with *Wurfkörper* (WK, or rocket launcher) and the fitting of four 21 cm *Wurfkörpen* was also considered. In February 1944, a WK 28 with a 'butterfly tail' was installed on Hs 129 B-2, W.Nr. 141689, and the machine was transferred to the test centre at Udetfeld for subsequent tests. On 20 May, an early production B-1 – its *Werknummer* recorded as 3393 (sic), an atypical number – was assigned to the III./LLG 1 (LLG for *Luftlandgeschwader*, or Air Landing Wing), for glider towing duty.

Besides weapons, the employment of larger bombs was also considered. In November, Hs 129 B-2, W.Nr. 0266, DQ+ZB, retained for earlier tests, was modified to carry 250 kg and 500 kg bomb loads. The following month, the same aircraft performed test flights with 4 x 50 kg bombs placed in various locations, while W.Nr. 140494 – the first to be equipped with the large 7.5 cm *BK 13* – fitted with various weapon combinations, took part in speed tests. Following the conclusion of the bomb load tests, the tail section of W.Nr. 0266 was subject to modifications. Both the rudder and elevator were enlarged to improve control. However, the August 1944 Henschel Monthly Report noted that the task could not be completed due to lack of airframe varnish. Subsequently, the work was halted the following month, before test flights could be carried out, and the aircraft was scrapped.

The Henschel team also experimented with an on-board Gero flame-thrower. The weapon was mounted under the fuselage and was supplied with inflammable liquid from a special tank. In the summer of 1944, an Hs 129 B-2 (W.Nr. 142001) was still under tests with this equipment. As late as 26 August, with the Henschel 129 weapons programme winding down, after completion of some revisions of the elevator, tailskid, and electrical equipment, this particular test aircraft had been transferred to the *E-Stelle* Munster-Nord at Faßberg for further tests. All test-bed aircraft were grounded the next month, then scrapped according to RLM instructions.

Other weapons experimentally fitted to the Hs 129 were the 70 mm 'Panzerblitz I.' and 55 mm 'Panzerblitz II.,' as well as 210 mm *Werfer Granate* W.Gr. 21 and 280 mm W. Gr. 28 un-guided rockets/grenades for the anti-tank role. A wide variety of other weapons and installations – such as the 300-litre jettisonable underbelly auxiliary fuel tank, or an ejection seat – were also experimentally built in to the Henschel Hs 129 and tested in both static and dynamic conditions.

An undated Henschel document, probably issued in mid-1943, mentions the following weapon configurations (again, without any particular *Rüstsatz* number being given), fitted to the Hs 129 B, for both field and test use:

Standardausrüstung (Standard Equipment):

Schußwaffen (armament):

1 x 3 cm MK 101, with 20 rounds, *Schuß-Trommel* (stored in a drum magazine); (later the same calibre, but improved) MK 103, with 30 rounds, *Gurtzuführung* (belt fed);
plus 2 x 15 mm MG 151, with 250 rounds each;
plus 2 x 7.8 mm MG 17, with 1000 rounds each;

Bomben (bombs):

4 x 50 kg C 50 under wing, *zusätzlich nur Bewaffnung* (employed together with main armament), or 8 x 50 kg C 50/ *bei Wegfall der Bewaffnung* (employed without main armament) MK 101 (103)

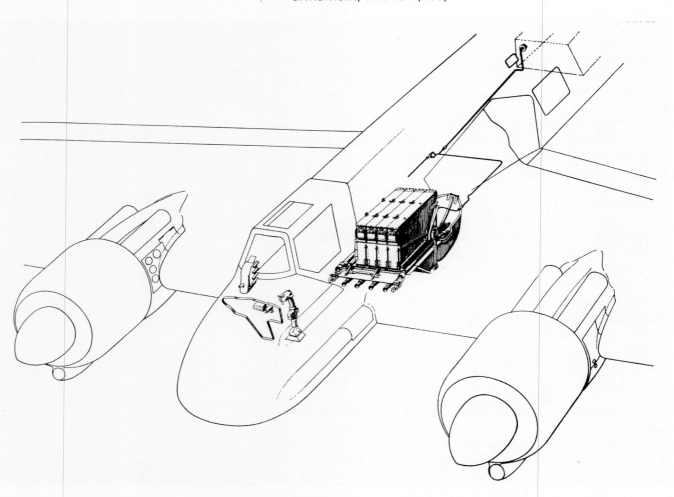

△ Handbook drawing showing layout of the 4 X MG 17 machine gun pack installation as installed to the Hs 129 B-1 and B-2.

Under development:

A *Rüstsatz* of 4 x MG 17, with 1000 rounds each;
B *Rüstsatz* of 2 x MG 131, with 500 rounds each
C *Rüstsatz* of 4 x MG 131, with 250 rounds each
D *Rüstsatz* of 2 x MG 151, with 250 rounds each
E *Rüstsatz* of 2 x 3 cm MK 103, with 25 rounds each (*Standbeschuß* – for firing at test range);
F *Einbau* (installation) of Rheinmetall MK (5cm) cannon, with 20 rounds;
G *Einbau* of [unspecified] 7.5 cm cannon, with a magazine developed by us (i.e., Henschel *Flugzeugwerk*), for 20 rounds (front use);

△ Another Rüstsatz (weapon kit) employed experimentally on the Hs 129 was made up from a battery of four 7.92 mm MG 17 machine guns, with 1000 rounds in each. The first Hs 129 B-1, W.Nr. 0151, KG+GI, was retained by Henschel for weapon tests.

◁▽ Two views showing the MG 17 machine-gun battery on its installation stand, as well as in the lowered position on the aircraft.

Advanced Weapon and Equipment Trials ○ **67**

▷ Another view showing the MG 17 machine gun battery in its installed position..

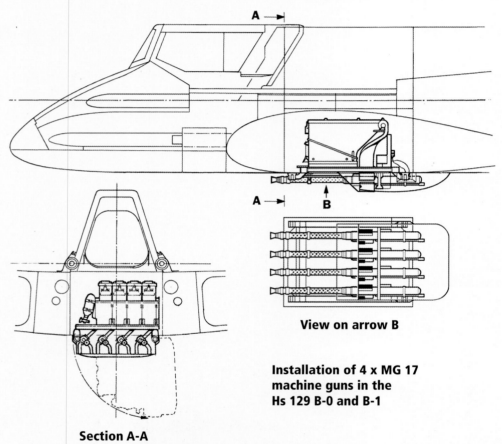

View on arrow B

Installation of 4 x MG 17 machine guns in the Hs 129 B-0 and B-1

Section A-A

H *Rüstsätze* of *Rost* 2 kg SD 24, 250 kg C250 and 500 kg C500 bombs (front use);

I *Einbau* of *Raketengeschossen sowohl unter Verwenung der Geschosse der Erdwaffe* (21 cm and 28 cm) *als auch Sondergeschossen der Luftwaffe* (5 cm and 7cm), *Truppenversuch* [employment of rocket-propelled projectiles, either together with the main armament (21 cm and 28 cm), or as a special armament (5 cm and 7 cm)];

J [description missing];

K *Einbau* of flame thrower, with a 300 litre tank (*Truppenversuch* - experiments on the field),

L *der Versuchseinbau für ein 6-Schuss-Magazin für 7.5cm Geschoss die senkrecht von oben beim Überfliegen des Zieles (Panzer) abgefeuert werden sollten. Die Auslösung des Schusses sollte automatisch durch Änderung der elektrischen Potentiallinien durch das Ziel vermittels einer vor dem Flugzeug angebrachten Antenne erfolgen. Die günstig verlaufenen Luftversuche wurden von der Luftfahrtforschungsanstalt Hermann Göring durchgeführt* (experimental construction of a launcher made up from six tubes, each housing a 7.5 cm diameter projectile. The projectiles would be automatically fired downwards when the target (an armoured vehicle) had been overflown at low altitude. The automatic triggering would be activated by the modification of the electro-magnetic field's potential lines generated by an antenna attached to the aircraft. This weapon had been tested with very good results at the Hermann Göring experimental test centre).

An interesting detail is included in various *Luftwaffe* aircraft loss records, in the form of a code placed after the sub-type: Hs 129 B-2/XVI ZS (three occurrences have been found so far: W.Nr. 141582, 141722 and 141875, all lost in combat in late 1944/early 1945). This suffix probably refers to the FuG 16 ZS radio set. This was a special version of the FuG 16 Z operating on a different frequency (40,3 - 44,7 MHz). It was fitted to ground support aircraft as a replacement for the standard FuG VIIa.

▽ Following the short A-0 pre-production series, 16 Argus As 410-powered A-1s were initially ordered from Henschel. This new batch was fitted with French Gnome-Rhône 14M 04/05 radial engines, driving three-bladed Ratier variable pitch metal propellers, and was subsequently renamed Hs 129 B-0. The order was then supplemented with the balance from the short-cut A-0 production, i.e. 11 aircraft, raising the total of B-0s variants to 27. The aircraft retained the A-0's flat plated double-slanted nose section, but the cockpit area had been upgraded, significantly increasing the pilot's all-around visibility. The first aircraft of this new batch (W.Nr. 0016, KK+VI) was modified to carry the downward firing SG 113A Förstersonde recoilless mortar shells situated in the fuselage centre-section. Note the nose-mounted 'T' shape antenna; this sensed the electro-magnetic field disturbances generated by a large metal mass when flying over an armoured fighting vehicle - triggering the mortars. Ironically, the Hs 129's main competitor, the Fw 189 can be seen in the background.

▷ Another view of the SG 113A Förstersonde, the vertically firing recoilless mortar installed in Hs 129 B-0, W.Nr. 0016. Interestingly the aircraft's Stammkennzeichen (radio call sign) KK+VI was not applied on the fuselage sides.

▽ Position of the Opta-Radio control box behind the pilot's seat.

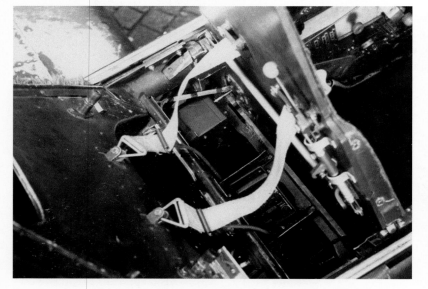

△ The size of the Opta-Radio control box as compared to a standard box of matches.

◁ The 7.5 mm, 1.5 kg mortar shell.

◁ An overhead view of the SG 113A Förstersonde as fitted to Hs 129 B-0, W.Nr. 0016.

◁△ Two colour photographs of the abandoned Hs 129 B-2, possibly W.Nr. 140499. This aircraft, along with two others, had been assigned to the experimental weapons programme, and equipped with the Förstersonde vertical firing mortar. Unfortunately, no further information is known about this particular aircraft, except that it was discovered by Allied troops at the Aeronautical Research Institute, located at Braunschweig/Volkenrode.

▽▷ Two photographs showing the installation of the SG 113 weapon in Hs 129 B-2, W.Nr. 0249. The photograph at right shows the fairing on the lower fuselage - through which the mortars fired.

▷ A close-up of the 'T' shaped nose-mounted target detection antenna.

◁◁△ A sequence of three photographs (viewed left to right) showing the approach and firing of the SG 113 weapon at a dummy target of a Soviet armoured vehicle.

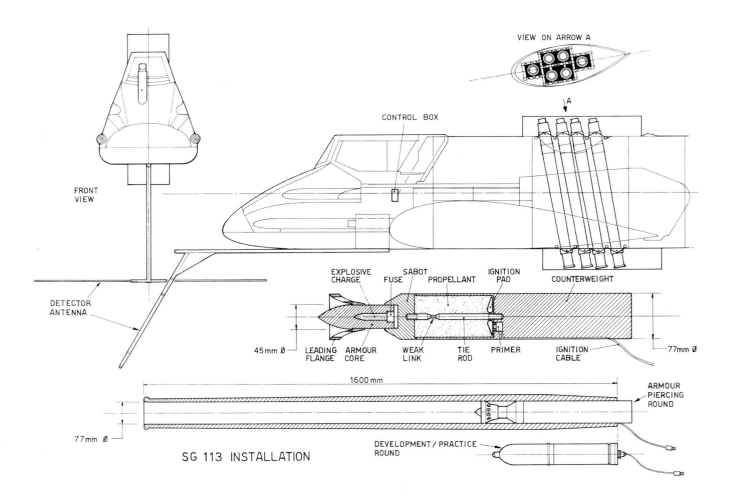

VIEW ON ARROW A

CONTROL BOX

FRONT VIEW

DETECTOR ANTENNA

EXPLOSIVE CHARGE   SABOT   IGNITION
FUSE   PROPELLANT   PAD   COUNTERWEIGHT

45mm Ø   LEADING   ARMOUR   WEAK   TIE   PRIMER   IGNITION   77mm Ø
          FLANGE   CORE   LINK   ROD   CABLE

1600 mm   ARMOUR
                                                            PIERCING
                                                            ROUND

77mm Ø

SG 113 INSTALLATION   DEVELOPMENT/PRACTICE
                             ROUND

B-3:
The Ultimate Gun Platform

" The penetration depth increased with the decrease of shooting range. This 'punch' was enough to knock out even the heaviest Soviet tank at the time, the 46 tonne IS-2 (Iosif Stalin 2)."

By early 1944, the *Luftwaffe* was calling for larger calibre airborne anti-tank weapons for use against the growing number of improved Soviet tanks and assault guns. The RLM requested that Henschel *Flugzeugwerk* study the feasibility of modifying the efficient 75 mm PaK 40L (*Panzerabwehrkanone*, or anti-tank cannon) for installation in the Hs 129. This gun was modified for aircraft use by adding a large muzzle brake for countering the weapon's recoil and by substituting the mechanical operation with an electro-pneumatic operation. This modified airborne weapon was designed as *Bordkanone BK* 7,5. The large calibre cannon had a muzzle velocity of 932.7 metres per second and could penetrate up to 130 mm of armour from 1000 metres at a 90 degree angle. If the projectile hit the target at a 30 degree angle, it was found that up to 95 mm of armour could be penetrated. The penetration depth increased with the decrease of the shooting range. This 'punch' was enough to knock out even the heaviest Soviet tank at that time, the 46 ton IS-2 (Iosif Stalin 2). The *BK* 7,5 had a rate of fire of 40 RPM (rounds per minute), which allowed the pilot to fire three or four rounds in a single pass on the target. Spent shell

casings and gun gases were ejected from a ventral gun housing. In case of emergency, the pilot could jettison the entire gun pack assembly, thus reduce weight and increase manoeuvrability.

Prolonged experiments with the huge *BK* 7,5 had shown that even with the heavy cannon mounted under the aircraft's centre section, flying performance was not significantly affected, except for some horizontal 'snaking' oscillations, which could be compensated. Extensive test firings showed also that this large calibre weapon could be successfully employed against virtually any existing moving targets. In January 1944, six series-built Hs 129 B-2s were designated to accommodate the centrally mounted *BK* 7,5, with a supply of 16 rounds in a *Trommelmagazin* (drum magazine), as well as two MG 131 machine guns mounted in the fuselage sides, each with 250 rounds (the pair of 20 mm cannon was deleted due to weight considerations). A new telescopic gun sight, called *Zielfernrohr* (Long-range/Telescopic Target Finding Scope) ZFR 3B, was to replace the previous Revi C 12, although it is unconfirmed that it was actually used in service. Since these were major changes, a new sub-version was allocated to the project: B-3.

Initially, a standard B-2 (W.Nr. 141258, BH+ZS) was fitted with a full-scale wooden mock-up of the *BK* 7,5, for in-flight test with the bulky weapon. The long cannon barrel protruded from the front of the aircraft, over one metre ahead of the nose. To study the airflow around the rear fuselage section, woollen tufts were attached to the airframe. Additionally, an extended vertical aerial was fitted to the windscreen top frame. The tests were carried out at *E-stelle* Travemünde and over the Baltic Sea in May 1944.

◁△ Far left and above, two views of Hs 129 B-2, W.Nr. 141258 coded BH+ZS, which was fitted with a wooden mock-up of the PaK 40 (BK 7.5 cm cannon) and fairing. The aircraft was used by the Erprobungsstelle to carry out trials over the Baltic Sea, to investigate its flight characteristics. Note the long vertical aerial mast above the canopy, which was linked to flight recorder equipment.

△ The final development of the Hs 129 was the C-1 sub-type, also known as the 'Cäsar'. The only C-1/V4, W.Nr. 220001, is depicted here, carrying the powerful 75 mm calibre BK 7.5 cannon, which was supplied with 16 rounds of ammunition fed from a drum magazine. The holes at the end of the barrel is a muzzle brake, which broke down the gases of the blast into smaller jets to avoid damage to the airframe and reduce the muzzle flash to the pilot. Due to weight restrictions, all fixed on-board weapons were apparently removed, the lower blast troughs being covered by a sheet metal fairing, while the upper troughs were simply left open with the holes plugged. After several test flights, the first – and only – Hs 129 C-1 was grounded at E-Stelle Tarnewitz on 13 July 1944, due to changes in aircraft production decisions.

▷ Handbook drawing of the BK 7.5 cm installation shown without the gun fairing for the standard Hs 129 B-3 variant.

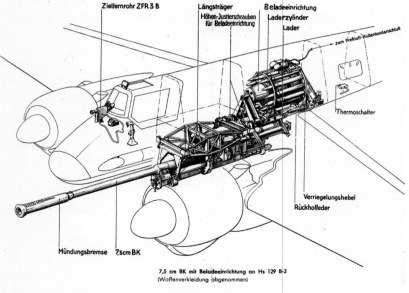

7,5 cm BK mit Beladeeinrichtung an Hs 129 B-3
(Waffenverkleidung abgenommen)

To compensate for the increased instability of the aircraft in flight and to tackle the 'snaking' oscillations during tracking trials, efforts were made to produce artificial in-flight stability. Two engineers from the DVL (*Deutsche Versuchsanstalt für Luftfahrt*, or German Aviation Testing Institute), Prof. K. H. Doetsch and his assistant, E. G. Friedrichs, split the rudder of a Hs 129 test aircraft horizontally into separate surfaces. The lower surface was mechanically tied to the rudder's pedals,

◁ A close-up view of the 75 mm PaK 40 fitted under an Hs 129. Not visible in this view is the magazine and the automatic loading mechanism housed inside the fuselage. The gun fairing has also been removed.

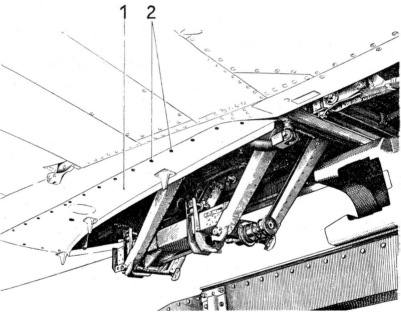

◁ **RLM drawing of the panels under the fuselage arround the mounting points for the 7.5 cm gun:**
1 – Cover panels
2 – Flush fixing screws

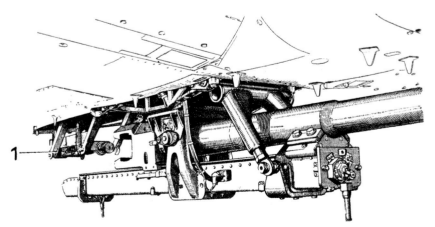

◁ **RLM drawing of the 7.5 cm gun installed:**
1 – Magazine carrier lowered

1

while the upper surface was controlled with an electromagnetic device fed by a yaw rate gyroscope. This ingenious solution was the first effective yaw damper, used after the war in the design of several combat aircraft (such as the US Navy Chance Vought F4U-5 Corsair fighter in 1949). The only available photograph of an operational B-3 does not show this solution was actually applied to series produced machines. Further improvements intended for the B-3 included additional armour protection around cockpit and engines.

By March reportedly only one B-2 had been fully converted to B-3 standard (W.Nr. 141292). This particular aircraft was transferred to the *E-Stelle* Tarnewitz on 23 June. The following month, on 8 July, another Hs 129 B-2, W.Nr. 141494, was fitted with the 7.5 cm *Bordkanone* and was sent to Tarnewitz. With this aircraft, single-shot air-to-ground firing trials were conducted by Rheinmetall-Borsig in August 1944. A third B-2 was also fully converted to the B-3 standard and subjected to various tests. The results of these firing trials were incorporated into the design of the B-3, which received minor reinforcements to the undersurface skin of the fuselage. Apparently, these particular test aircraft were not renamed B-3, but kept their original designation and construction numbers. The official Henschel monthly reports referred to them as B-3s converted from B-2s.

◁ **Shells lying in outer ring of drum:**
1 – Front guide rail
2 – Shell

The first true B-3 (W.Nr. 162033, DT+GB) rolled off the production line at the end of July 1944 [DT+GA was a Ju 52]. It was followed by three others (W.Nr. 162034 to 162036, DT+GC to DT+GE) the next month. The three initial aircraft were recorded as being ferried to the *Erprobungsstelle Tarnewitz* in August (*Oblt.* Gatzemeier flew DT+GB to Tarnewitz on 11 August), from where they were directed towards *Erprobungs-kommando 26* (Test and Evaluation Detachment 26) on 25 August. This special unit had been formed from 11.(Pz)/SG 9 on 29 December 1943, with the designated base at the airfield of *E-Stelle Udetfeld*. At that time, the strength was made up of 12 aircraft comprising four Hs 129s, four Fw 190s and four Ju 87s, along with a liaison Bf 108 and a transport aircraft. The unit was disbanded on 14 February 1945, the personnel and aircraft – including an unspecified number of Hs 129s – being transferred under command of the *General der Schlachtflieger*, which, in turn, reassigned them to an *Ergänzungsstaffel* of SG 151. Earlier, the Hs 129s were tested at *Erprobungskommando Hs 129*, based at Braunschweig-Waggum, in 1941/1942.

Production of the B-3 was abruptly halted in August 1944 by the *Rüstungsstab*, due to a drastic shift in production goals set up by the hard-pressed RLM. By then, 20 units had been delivered (the last 16 units received the *Werknummer range* 162037-162052). These airframes were fitted with 40 of the 47

△ **BK 7.5 instrument panel in cockpit:**
1 – Safety switch
2 – Weapon selection lever
3 – Firing button
4 – Arming switch
5 – Gunsight dimmer switch

△ A rare photograph showing an operational Hs 129 B-3, after being abandoned on the field in the face of the advancing Red Army. This is one of two only known photographs (see next page) showing an Hs 129 B-3, equipped with the 75 mm BK 7.5 underbelly cannon, in operational service. W.Nr. 162052 was part of IV.(Pz.)/SG 9 when it was captured near Schippenbeil (today Sepopol, Poland), south-east of Königsberg (today Kaliningrad, Russia), in December 1944.

more powerful Gnome-Rhône 14 M 38 engines that were available at the factory. The remaining engines were used for supply purposes. According to the strict order arriving from Berlin – included in the August 1944 Henschel Monthly Report – all other airframes and airframe parts were to be scrapped. Only a small portion of the existing stock was to be retained for the supply of spares for the operational aircraft. Thus, in total, 23 aircraft fitted to B-3 standards existed, 20 newly manufactured and three upgraded examples.

Most B-3s went directly for combat duty with the 13.(Pz)/ SG 9 (which received the first five B-3s in September) and the 14. *Staffel* of the same *Gruppe* (which received its first B-3 also in September). A few were assigned to piloting schools (*Oblt*. Gatzemeier flew DT+GD to Udetfeld, today the International Airport of Katowice in Upper Silesia / Poland, on 27 September). Two were retained by Henschel *Flugzeugwerk* for an unspecified *Umbau* task. The last operational B-3s were still reported as extant with 10.(Pz) and 14./SG 9 on 9 April 1945. In the last *Luftwaffe* aircraft strength returns report sent to Berlin, 19 B-2s and B-3s were listed with these two *Schlachtstaffeln*, making a last stand in western Hungary (based at Veszprém) and in Upper Silesia (based at Weidengut, today Wierzbie, Poland), respectively.

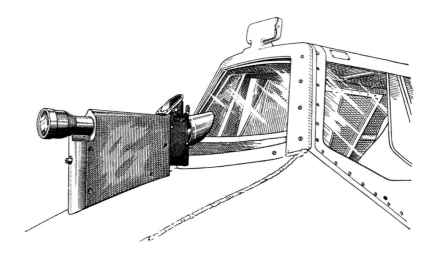

◁ The ZFR 3 A telescopic gunsight.

△ Another view of the abandoned Hs 129 B-3, W.Nr. 162052 of IV. (Pz.)/SG 9 when it was captured near Schippenbeil in December 1944. It does not seem to have been fitted with an enlarged rudder, as planned for the late-production Hs 129s carrying the BK 7.5 cannon. Additionally the rudder is not split horizontally, as was done experimentally at the DVL, to compensate for the increased instability due to the fitting of the cannon.

Final Developments

" Besides employing more powerful engines, the Henschel design team developed a series of aerodynamic refinements of the airframe, intended to be implemented in the new version of the Hs 129. "

Another sub-type was also considered by the Henschel design team to replace the B-2/B-3. This new version, the C-1 – C for *Cäsar* – was to be armed with two remotely-controlled 30 mm MK 103 guns under the fuselage, placed side-by-side, on a special mounting. Each gun would have had a 60-round magazine – in contrast to only 30 rounds available for the single MK 101/103 fitted to the B-2. The pilot remotely controlled these weapons, which had limited traverse (side-by-side) rotation. Completing the main armament were the regular weapons existing in the B-2 – two pairs of fixed, forward-firing MG 17s and MG 151/20s – as well as two fixed MG 17s, firing rearwards. These additional machine guns were considered to offer defence capability against enemy aircraft attacking from the rear, eliminating the dangerous blind spot existing in the 'B' series. The pilot was to be provided with a rear-view Revi 5 gunsight for aiming these machine guns.

This gunsight was tested on a standard Hs 129 B-2, W.Nr. 0224, DE+ZR, at the *E-Stelle* Tarnewitz during 1943. New bomb shackles with increased capacity, suitable for bombs up to 1000 kg and to be used instead of the pair of underbelly cannon, were also considered.

Originally, not only was the armament intended to be changed, but also the aircraft's main impediment: the engines. The replacement engine type intended for the C-1 was yet another of foreign manufacture – due to the lack of readily available suitable German powerplants – the upgraded Italian Isotta-Fraschini *'Delta'* 12-cylinder, air-cooled engine, rated at 1200 hp (895 kW) max. output at take-off (data from German source). The Isotta-Fraschini *'Delta'* radial suffered through lengthy development problems, but was promised to be available in the short term. However, political considerations and the unexpected turn of events (*i.e.*, the Italian armistice of 3 September 1943), ended the finalisation of this project. As a stopgap measure, an advanced version of the Gnome-Rhône R14 radial was chosen instead. The R14 M38 offered increased output, 820 hp (611.5 kW), instead of 700 hp (522 kW) given by the regular G&R R14 M04/05. The added engine power assured 50 km/h extra speed to the planned new sub-type (compared to the B-2). However, overall take-off weight – including the additional on-board weapons – increased by 200 kg. Reportedly, a series-produced B-2, W.Nr. 0267, DQ+ZC, was re-engined with this new powerplant when performing its maiden flight in August 1943, with satisfactory results. However, the tests ran into problems, though not because of the new powerplants. In September the aircraft collided with a Junkers Ju 88 bomber and was damaged. Once repaired, carburettor problems arose. It flew again in November and December, but the carburettor problems persisted. In January 1944, the test aircraft was grounded, and the engines removed as they were needed for the new C-1 prototype. The aircraft returned from the Rechlin

testing grounds to the HFW where it was subsequently repaired. Once serviceable, it was flown back to *E-Stelle* Rechlin on 3 August for further tests. However, the aircraft returned to Schönefeld the following month, for removal of its TEV calibration unit, and was subsequently deactivated due to the halt in the Hs 129 programme.

Besides employing more powerful engines, the Henschel design team developed a series of aerodynamic refinements of the airframe, intended to be implemented in the new version of the Hs 129. These improvements included form-pressed armour plates, bent and curved to the final aerodynamic shape, thus eliminating the light-metal plates used as outside covers, employed on the 'B' series to give the aircraft the required contour. This would have resulted in a lighter airframe and reduced manufacturing costs. The engine cowling and oil radiators were also to be redesigned, in order to improve aerodynamic efficiency and to achieve a better airflow over the wing surfaces. Experiments to test all such proposed modifications were carried out with an airframe mock-up in a wind tunnel. However, although these proposals indicated that significant improvements would be achieved, it was considered the results did not justify the necessary retooling and disruption to the manufacturing process, which would result and would only have been implemented had the new Italian or other high-

△ A photograph of the Revi 5 rear-view periscope gun sight which was intended to assist the pilot in aiming the two rearward firing 7.92 mm MG 17 machine guns which were planned to be installed on the mid-fuselage sides of the Hs 129 C, as a defence measure against attacks from the rear. As a flying test aircraft for the gunsight, an early Hs 129 B-2, coded DE+ZR, W.Nr.0224, based at the E-Stelle Tarnewitz, was used.

performance engines become available. Since the supply of these engines did not materialize, further development of the Hs 129 was therefore restricted solely to the armament.

After a few test flights, the first – and only – true Hs 129 C-1/V4, W.Nr. 220001, the fourth Hs 129 prototype, was grounded at *E-Stelle* Tarnewitz on 13 July 1944. The September 1944 Henschel Monthly Report noted that the V4 was deactivated, then scrapped.

At an unspecified date in early 1944, the RLM issued a special order calling for 150 Hs 129 Cs. The *'Reduziertes Jägerstab Flugzeugprogramm'* (Reduced Fighter Aircraft Programme) No. 22.14, issued on 3 June, prescribed an increase in Hs 129 B/C output. Production of the new sub-version, the B-3, started in July. It was planned to be only a short run, until production could switch to the improved C-1. A significant number of B-3 and C-1 airframes were completed or were in the process of manufacture by August 1944, when production was suddenly halted by the RLM. Officially, this happened due to the unsatisfactory test results of the large-calibre *Bordkanone*.

▷ The Revi 5 rear-view periscope gun sight.

△ Another view of the base of the Revi 5 rear-view periscope gun sight.

In reality, however, the production halt occurred due to shifting priorities in aircraft types required by the RLM's new aircraft production programme, called the *'Blitzbomber Programm'*. Accordingly, the Henschel comapny was instructed to cease immediately manufacture of the Hs 129, and change tooling for the mass production under licence of the Ju 388 twin-engine advanced bomber. At that point, over 100 more-or-less completed Hs 129 B-2, B-3 and C-1 airframes existed at Henschel *Flugzeugwerk* plants. Four B-2s and 16 B-3s were still completed and handed over to the *Luftwaffe* in the last production month, while some partially finished airframes and main parts had been used to repair and refurbish damaged aircraft. However, the majority of the airframes had to be scrapped – including all *Cäsars* – causing a 35 million *Reichsmark* loss to the *Henschel Flugzeugwerk AG*.

Sudden demise of a Tank Killer

"... According to the current plan, the aircraft type will be superseded by April 1945. The reason for the phase-out is due to the high fuel consumption."

▽ An early production Hs 129 B-2 being prepared for a sortie against Soviet targets in the Kuban, in May 1943, along with the Staffel's other Schlachtflugzeuge. Note 'Red F' of 8.(Pz.)/Sch.G.1, has three white tank 'kill' markings painted on the rudder.

In August 1944, all ongoing work on the Hs 129 was halted by the RLM. Concomitantly, all existing test aircraft, involved in various weapon experiments, were also grounded, then scrapped. The October 1944 Henschel Monthly Report concisely noted *"...the last aircraft after the cancellation of the programme has been delivered. Plant No. 2 is to be closed down. The repair for the Hs 129 at home [at the factory] will be discontinued, effective immediately. Aircraft arriving for repair are to be scrapped. Frontline repairs are to be performed only by the units. According to the current plan, the aircraft type will be superseded by April 1945. The reason for the phase-out is the excessive fuel consumption."*

This marked the end of the six-year-long Hs 129 programme. In October 1944, the last B-3s were delivered to a specialized *Luftwaffe* anti-tank unit active on the Eastern Front, namely the 13 and 14. *Staffeln* of *Schlachtgeschwader* 9. One of these, W.Nr. 162052 - the very last Hs 129 to be actually delivered to the *Luftwaffe* for combat operations – was captured by advancing Soviet troops at Schippenbeil (today Sepopol, Poland), south-east of Königsberg (today Kaliningrad, Russia), in December 1944.

Summing up the overall Hs 129 production figures from September 1940 to September 1944, according to the author's calculations, it appears that a grand total of approximately 1,168 units (including all prototypes, pre-series and series-manufactured aircraft, those written off during Allied bombings and also the 100-plus airframes scrapped in late 1944 when production was halted, as well as the exports to Rumania) had

◁ Probably the same 'Red F' as opposite, is caught by the camera on a low-level pass over an airfield. The underbelly cannon is present, but no bombs were carried during this photo session. The lower part of the main wheels stick out from the undercarriage bay, facilitating an eventual belly landing, restricting damage to the airframe. The incomplete Stammkennzeichen reads G?+KZ.

altogether been manufactured at Henschel *Flugzeugwerke'* Schönefeld and Johannisthal Plants. An official post-war Henschel publication, titled *'Sonderdruck der Henschel Flugzeugwerke GmbH'* (Special Publication of the Henschel Aircraft Factory Ltd.), published by the HFW's successor company in Kassel, gives the total number of series-manufactured Hs 129s as 1160 – without giving any further production details – a number similar to the author's calculations. However, the number of combat-ready aircraft of the 'B' series, accepted by the *Luftwaffe* for combat operations was certainly less, believed to be just over 1000 units – contrary to the 866, 875 or 876 units of the 'B' sub-version, put forward in the majority of published sources. Additionally, 145 Hs 129s were repaired at Henschel *Flugzeugwerke* Johannisthal works, between June 1942 and August 1944, which were then returned to service.

By studying accessible *Werk-nummer* sequences assigned to the Hs 129, and available *Luftwaffe* and ARR loss data, pilots' log books and export data, it can be ascertained that the overall actual production figure was significantly higher than 890 or 894 aircraft as is usually mentioned by various primary and secondary sources. This discrepancy cannot yet be fully explained, due to the lack of crucial documents destroyed close to or shortly after the war's end, or removed by the occupying Soviet troops. The final answer might very well lie in one of the ex-Soviet archives in Russia.

▽ This winter photograph depicts 'Yellow 4' boxed between Ju 88s at Orsha South airfield, located in Western Byelorussia, in late 1942. The straight antenna mast, the circular air intake underneath the engine cowling and the landing light mounted in the port wing's leading edge identify it as an Hs 129 B-1. As Zusätzliche Ausrüstung (Auxiliary Equipment), a 30 mm MK 101 cannon is mounted under the fuselage, in a streamlined gondola, complementing the two ETC 50 under wing bomb racks fitted as Ständige Ausrüstung (Standard Equipment).

Henschel Hs 129 Production List (Reconstruction)

No.	Werknummer	Sub-version	Delivery Month	Reconstructed Stammkennzeichen	Notes
1	129 3001	Hs 129 V1	May 1939	D-ONUD TF+AM	Original Henschel *Projekt* P 46. Delayed due to lack of Argus engine and propeller. *Flugklar* 12 May 1939. First flight 26 May 1939. Presented to Hitler 3 July 1939. Test flown at *E-Stelle* Tarnewitz on 24 April 1940 by *Oblt.* Gatzemeier transferred to *E-Stelle* Rechlin 14 December 1940.
1	129 3002	Hs 129 V2	November 1939	TF+AN (not used)	Delayed due to lack of Argus engine and propeller. One Argus 410 engine arrived in July 1939. The other removed from V1. First flight 30 Nov. 1939. Crashed 5 January 1940.
1	129 3003	Hs 129 V3	April 1940	TF+AO	Delayed due to lack of Argus engine and propeller. First flight 2 April 1940. At *E-Stelle* Rechlin on 31 May 1940. In October 1940 rebuilt as prototype for the B series (G&R radial engine) and renamed V3/U-1. First flight with new powerplant 19 March 1941. Used as testbed at Henschel. Scrapped July 1944.
12	129 3004-129 3015	Hs 129 A-0	September 1940-May 1941	GM+OA to GM+OL	First flight of 129 3004 on 1 August. 1940. Temporary (reusable) ferry code for 129 3008-129 3015 HS+MB (HS for Henschel). (GM+OM and 'ON were assigned to Hs 130s). Most A-0s tested with *Erprobungskommando Hs 129*, based at Braunschweig-Waggum, throughout 1941, then at Lippstadt, in the first half of 1942.
(60)	(0101-0160)	Hs 129 A-1	(May 1941-December 1941)	N/A	Initially designated Hs 129 A-1/14M. Production cancelled November 1940. Ten already manufactured units (W.Nr. 0151-0160) renamed B-1.
27	0016-0042	Hs 129 B-0	August 1941-1942	KK+VI to KK+VZ (0016 to 0033)	Originally intended as A-1s. Re-engined with Gnome-Rhône 14M and renamed B-0. The balance of 11 aircraft from the reduced A-0 order added to the originally ordered 16 aircraft, raising the total to 27 B-0s. W.Nr. 0018 test flown by *Gefr.* Siegfried Schuricht at Braunschweig, from 27 September 1941 on. W.Nr. 0039 and 0042 flown repeatedly by the same pilot at Tatsinskaya, USSR, in July and August 1942 as member of Stab. III/*Zerstörerschule* 2.
10	0151-0160	Hs 129 B-1	December 1941-March 1942	KG+GI to KG+GR	Initially designated Hs 129A-1/14M. Last 10 planned A-1s re-engined with Gnome-Rhône 14M and renamed B-1. W.Nr. 0159 first flown in combat by *Fw.* Arno Ehrhardt at Soldatskaya on 25 October 1942.
40	0161-0200	Hs 129 B-1	March 1942-May 1942		Originally 60 B-1s ordered (W.Nr. 0151-0210). Last ten air frames (W.Nr. 0201- 0210) upgraded to B-2 standards (see below). W.Nr. 0167 flown by *Fw.* Paul Krieg at Deblin-Irena on 20 August 1943.
(250)	(0201-0450)	Hs 129 B-1 trop	(December 1941-April 1942)	N/A	Tropicalised version, cancelled April 1942. Production instead as B-2.
250	0201-0450	Hs 129 B-2	May 1942-March 1943	GD+ZA to GD+ZB (0221 to 0222); DE+ZQ to DE+ZZ (0223 to 0232); DQ+ZA to DQ+ZZ (0265 to 0290); GD+CA to GD+CT (0291 to 0310); CH+SD to CH+SX (0311 to 0331); GG+EE to GG+EX (0332 to 0351); VE+NA to VE+NS (0352 to 0370); PG+MH to PG+MZ (0371 to 0389); SJ+WA to SJ+WT (0411 to 0430);	First ten airframes were the last ten B-1s, upgraded to B-2 standards. 0266 and 0267 kept at HFW for testing. Engines of 0266 used for C-1/V4. Henschel document: in August 1942, the 100th series production Hs 129 B delivered to the front, 16 already lost by then.

No.	Werknummer	Sub-version	Delivery Month	Reconstructed Stammkennzeichen	Notes
10+	140363 - 140372*	Hs 129 B-2	1943		140363 and 140372 in ARR (Royal Rumanian Air Force) service. * Production block probably larger.
40	140401-140440	Hs 129 B-2	March 1943-April 1943		
50	140491-140540	Hs 129 B-2	April 1943-May 1943	DO+XD to DO+XZ (140491 to 140513);	140494 tested with BK 5 & BK 13 cannon in December 1943 and July 1944.
130	140711-140840	Hs 129 B-2	May 1943	GL+PA to GL+PW (140721 to 140743); NN+KA to NN+KW (140788 to 140810);	March 1943: 331 Hs 129 Bs delivered to the front, 212 already lost. W.Nr. 140728 ferried by Fw. Arno Ehrhardt from the Johannisthal Plant to Krakow on 25 May 1943.
30	140861-140890	Hs 129 B-2	1943		
1+	141068	Hs 129 B-2	1943		141068 in ARR service. Does not fit into any reconstructed production block.
20	141111-141130	Hs 129 B-2	1943		September 1943: 560 Hs 129Bs delivered to the front, 383 already lost.
100	141201-141300	Hs 129 B-2	1943-1944	BH+ZB to BH+ZZ (141241 to 141265);	141291 & 141292 tested with BK 5 cannon in December 1943. Test with Flak 18 cancelled. Tests with BK 7,5 successful. Finally, 141291, 141292 & 140494 equipped with BK 7,5 (to B-3 standard). 140494 & 141291 transferred to E-Stelle Tarnewitz in July 1944. December 1943: 664 Hs 129 Bs delivered to the front, 495 already lost.
1+	141335	Hs 129 B-2	N/A		In Luftwaffe service. Crashed 50 percent on 8 November 1943. Does not fit into any reconstructed production block.
40	141371-141410	Hs 129 B-2	1944		141410 is shown as '1410' in Jupp Oehl's Flugbuch as flown in combat on 21 October 1944.
1+	141433	Hs 129 B-2	1944		141433 in ARR service. Does not fit into any reconstructed production block.
100	141491-141590	Hs 129 B-2	1944	SS+LA to SS+LJ (141581 to 141590);	
80	141681-141760	Hs 129 B-2	1944	NK+DA to NK+DY (141711 to 141735);	
70	141821-141890	Hs 129 B-2	1944	RU+PA to RU+PX (141837 to 141860); SR+JA to SR+JT (141861 to 141880);	
50+	141961-142011	Hs 129 B-2	1944		142001 equipped with flamethrower, transferred to E-Stelle Munster-North Fassberg, 26 August 1944.
50	142041-142090	Hs 129 B-2	1944		Production block also given as from 142031 to 142100 (70 aircraft).
32	162001-162032	Hs 129 B-2	June 1944-August 1944		Production halted in August 1944, all extant airframes scrapped.
20	162033-162052	Hs 129 B-3	July 1944-August 1944	DT+GB to DT+GU	Production halted in August 1944, all extant airframes scrapped. Last production unit, 162052, captured by the Soviets (photo). DT+GB test flown at E-Stelle Tarnewitz on 11 August 1944 by Oblt. Gatzemeier. DT+GD ferry flight from Breslau to Udetfeld on 27 September 1944. (DT+GA was a Ju 52).
1	220001	Hs 129 C-1/V-4	N/A		4th and final prototype. On 13 July 1944: Stillgelegt (grounded). First of eight planned C-1s. Production cancelled 7 March 1944. All extant airframes scrapped in September 1944.
Total* 1168+					*As reconstructed by the author, based on available information. Actual production figure could be somewhat higher (a post war Henschel document mentions a total of 1160 'B' versions built). Published production/acceptance total is only 894 Hs 129s (all prototypes and variants). A total of 145 Hs 129s were also repaired at Henschel Flugzeugwerk between June 1942-September 1944.

Other Stammkennzeichen with unidentified Werknummern correlation (sub-version given where known): BQ+TX (B-2), CC+IN to 'IO, CD+ZR (B-1), CE+MN, CG+UK to 'UR (B-2), CH+CW, CI+TI (B-2), CS+UL to 'UV (B-2), DE+JR, DI+VG to 'VH, DL+PU to 'PX (B-2), DN+ME (B-2), G?+KZ (B-2), GE+MN (B-2), GE+SG to 'SS (B-2), GU+OD, HI+JH (B-2), KC+QW (B-2), KF+DH to 'DX (B-2), KL+SA (B-2), PH+UC (W.Nr.XXX407) to 'UR (B-2), RS+OD (B-2), SS+JB to 'JR (B-2), SX+BH (B-2), VE+ZG (B-2).

List of aircraft variants in use and flight statistics for Hs 129

January 1944

Hs 129 A-1   4 Aircraft for training, 14 hours of serviceability, 111 total number of flights made
Hs 129 B-2   18 Aircraft for training, 236 hours of serviceability, 545 total number of flights made
Hs 129 B-2   117 Aircraft with operational units, 967 hours of serviceability, 1,493 total number of flights made
Hs 129 B-2   5 Aircraft at *E-Stelle* Rechlin Test Centre, 3 hours of serviceability, 17 total number of flights made

Total: 4 Hs 129 A-1 [sic!], 0 Hs 129 B-1 and 140 Hs 129 B-2

August/September 1944

Hs 129 B-1 & B-2 5 Aircraft for training, --- hours flying, --- total number of flights
Hs 129 B-1 & B-2 92 Aircraft with operational units, 673 hours of flying, 1,208 total number of flights
Hs 129 B-1 & B-2 8 Aircraft with various test centres (e.g. E-Stelle Rechlin), 1 hour flying time, 2 flights made
Hs 129 B-1 & B-2 20 Aircraft being serviced and in reserve, 41 hours flying, 65 total number of flights made
Hs 129 B-3   1 Aircraft with operational unit, --- hours flying, --- total number of flights made
Hs 129 B-3   2 Aircraft being serviced and in reserve, 2 hours flying, 2 total number of flights made

Total: 0 Hs 129 A, 125 Hs 129 B-1 & B-2 and 3 Hs 129 B-3

△ A dramatic photograph taken of 'Red G', a late production Hs 129 B-2, coming in to land on an airfield in Lithuania, in the summer of 1944. The black D painted over the yellow rear fuselage band – Eastern Front Theatre identification – was the last letter of the aircraft's four-letter Stammkennzeichen. Note the worn appearance of this Henschel. At this stage of the war, only the white outline of the fuselage and upper wing Balkenkreuz was applied directly over the camouflage colours. The lower wing Balkenkreuz and tail Hakenkreuz remained unchanged. During the last months of the war, the latter two markings were also simplified.

Appendix 3

Basic Specifications of the Hs 129 A-0

Wingspan:	14.20 m
Length:	9.75 m
Height:	3.25 m
Wing area:	28.40 m^2
Empty Weight:	3260 kg
Maximum Weight:	4310 kg
Powerplant:	two Argus As 410A-1 air-cooled engines, with 12 cylinders in 60 degrees inverted 'V' configuration, of max. 465 h.p. (346 kW) output at 3100 rpm, driving Argus-Automatisch two-blade, variable-pitch, metal propellers
Armament:	two 7.9 mm MG 17 machine guns and two 20 mm MG 151 cannon, built into the front part of the fuselage, complemented by four 50 kg bombs or two S125 *Nebelgeräte* (instead of bombs)
Radio Equipment:	FuG XVII
Maximum Speed:	354 km/h
Service Ceiling:	5400 m
Range:	650 km
Crew:	One

led Specifications of the Hs 129 B-0/B-1/B-2 (from factory manuals)

Armoured ground attack aircraft, for low level and dive-bombing missions, carried out with machine guns, cannon and bombs against ground targets, and with MK 101 cannon mounted as conversion kit against armoured targets [B-1 & B-2 only]. Can also be employed as armed reconnaissance aircraft in a secondary rôle

Hs 129 B-0 (*Werknummer* 0016-0042)
Hs 129 B-1 (*Werknummer* 0151-0200)
Hs 129 B-2 (from *Werknummer* 0201)
Hs 129 B-2 trop. (fitted with tropical *Rüstsatz* - conversion kit). Cancelled

Crew:	One (pilot)
Construction:	Twin-engine, low-wing, cantilever monoplane with all-metal airframe
Wings:	Two-spar, all-metal construction, with stressed skin covering. Centre section, carrying the two engine nacelles, built integrally with the fuselage. Two tapering outer sections, built separately, each weighing 122 kg. Straight leading edge and swept forward trailing edge from root to tip. Entire trailing edge hinged, the outer sections acting as slotted ailerons, while the inner sections as slotted flaps.
Fuselage:	Truncated triangle cross section structure with the wing root and centre sections built into the broad base. Nose section made of spot welded 6 to 12 mm thick armour plate, the remainder of light metal stressed skin construction. Total weight of armoured forward fuselage section, including cockpit 'bathtub' 469 kg. The fuselage centre section of riveted light alloy structure was attached to forward fuselage section by bolts. Weight of fuselage centre section with wing inner sections and nacelles 1063 kg. Rear fuselage section with the tail unit light metal alloy structure.
Landing gear:	Single-wheel retractable type. The single-leg main unit retracts hydraulically backwards into the lower engine nacelle. A part of the wheel protrudes slightly from the nacelle, when raised, to help during force-landing. Non-retractable, single-leg tail wheel.
Powerplant:	2 x French-made Gnome & Rhône 14 M 04/05, 14-cylinder air-cooled twin-radial, with a compressor set for full compression to 4000 m height. '04' denotes counter-clockwise turning engine, mounted on the port nacelle, while '05' clockwise turning engine, mounted on starboard nacelle. Weight of complete engine nacelle 589 kg. Bottom of cowling protected by 5 mm armour plate. 700 hp (522 kW) output at take-off, at 1.5 ata pressure and 3030 RPM. 770 hp (574 kW) max. output in emergency situation, at 1.5 ata pressure and 3030 RPM. 650 hp (488 kW) output in combat situation, at 1.2? pressure and 2750 RPM. 455 hp (339 kW) output while cruising, at grou? 1.1 ata pressure and 2350 RPM. 515 hp (384 kW) output while cruising, at ? pressure and 2350 RPM.
Propeller:	2 x three-blade automatic French-ma? electrically operated constant spee? electrically adjustable pitch to the R? degrees limits. Diameter: 2.60 m [B-0?

Fuel Tanks:	2 x wing tanks with 205-litre capacity each. One fuselage tank with 200-litre capacity
Oil Tanks:	2 x wing tanks with 35-litre capacity each
Fuel Grade:	Aircraft gasoline, 87 octane, B 4
Oil Grade:	Aero Shell
Hydraulic Oil Grade:	Shell AB 11
Radio Set/Locator:	FuG 17 & FuG 25 [B-0] FuG 7a (B-1 & B-2 to Werknummer 330) FuG 16 ZF (B-2 from Werknummer 331)
Armament (fixed):	2 x 7.92 mm MG 17 machine guns with 1000 rounds 2 x 20 mm MG 151/20 cannon with 250 rounds
Armament (drop):	2 x ETC 50 on outer wing undersurfaces
Rüstsatz 1:	4 x ETC 50 (under fuselage)
Rüstsatz 2:	1 x ETC 500 (under fuselage)
Rüstsatz 3:	1 x MK 101 with 30 rounds in T30 drum magazine (under fuselage)
Rüstsatz 4:	1x RB 20/30 or RB 7/9 automatic photo camera
Gunsight:	Revi C12c
Electrical system:	24 Volts, supplied by a generator and battery. This system powered all on-board gauges, instruments, radio equipment, etc. Armament was also electrically operated.

Technical specifications:

Wingspan:	14.20 m
Length:	9.82 m
Height (on ground):	3.42 m
Height (horizontal):	4.01 m

Fuselage max. cross section (width): 1.10 m
Fuselage max. cross section (height): 1.16 m

Main wheel span:	4.03 m
Wing area:	29.00 m^2
Wing root cord width:	2.90 m
Wing loading:	171 kg/m^2 [B-0], 173 kg/m2 [B-1 & B-2]
Weight/power ratio:	3.55 kg/hp [B-0], 3.59 kg/hp [B-1 & B-2]
Power/wing area ratio:	48.3 hp/m^2

Maximum speed:	345 km/h (at ground level),
	360 km/h (at 1000 m),
	374 km/h (at 2000 m),
	388 km/h (at 3000 m),
	403 km/h (at 4000 m)
	[Note: max. speeds are approx. 20 km/h higher when flying without bomb load]
Cruising speed:	316 km/h (at ground level),
	331 km/h (at 1000 m),
	346 km/h (at 2000 m),
	361 km/h (at 3000 m),
	376 km/h (at 4000 m)
Take-off speed:	144 km/h
Landing speed:	145 km/h
Range (at cruising speed):	555 km (flying at ground level),
	570 km (flying at 1000 m),
	585 km (flying at 2000 m),
	600 km (flying at 3000 m),
	620 km (flying at 4000 m)

▽ This photograph shows Hs 129 B-2, W.Nr. 0297 after restoration to flying condition in RAF colours and markings (NF756) with No.1426 Flight at RAF Collyweston in 1944. This aircraft was formerly Blue 'C' of 4.(Pz)/Sch.G2 which was captured in Libya, North Africa.

Taxiing distance for take-off (loaded 4900 kg):
320 m

Distance to reach 20 m height (loaded 4900 kg):   510 m

Taxiing distance during landing (loaded 4500 kg):   370 m

Distance from 20 m height to standstill (loaded 4500 kg):   650 m

Flying on one engine, while fully loaded: possible up to 3000 m

Empty weight: 3675 kg [B-0], 3681 kg [B-1 & B-2]

Take-off weight: 4583 kg (fully armed, without bombs) [B-0],
                       4871 kg (fully armed, incl. MK 101, without bombs) [B-1 & B-2],
                       4910 kg (fully armed, with 6 x 50 kg bombs) [B-0],
                       4964 kg (fully armed, with 6 x 50 kg bombs) [B-1 & B-2],
                       4972 kg (fully armed, with 144 x 2 kg bombs) [B-0],
                       4984 kg (fully armed, incl. MK 101, with 2 x 50 kg bombs)
                       [B-1 & B-2],
                       4952 kg (fully armed, with 4 x MK 17 and 2 x AB 24
                       bomb containers) [B-1 & B-2],
                       5003 kg (fully armed, with 6 x AB 24 bombs containers)
                       [B-1 & B-2],
                       5019 kg (fully armed, with 1 x 250 kg bomb & 4 x 50 kg bombs)
                       [B-1 & B-2],

Service Ceiling: 4000 m

Note: It is worthwhile comparing these optimal factory data with the practical operational data collected by the Rumanian ground-attack units in field conditions (see Appendix 4).

◁△ All that is left today of Henschel's rugged Schlachtflugzeug, is this nose section, formerly belonging to Hs 129 B-2, W.Nr. 0385. This particular aircraft, operated by 8.(Pz)/SchG.2, coded 'Blue G', was captured by US forces in Tunisia, North Africa, after it was left behind at Toubakeur airfield, in the spring of 1943. Later on, it was transported to the USA, where it received FE-4600 (foreign equipment) code. Damaged in a landing in the US in 1946, it was subsequently sold for scrap. Currently it is stored in Australia undergoing restoration as a complete unit. The Hs 129's nose section incorporated an armoured 'bathtub', to protect the pilot from ground fire. The thickness of the armour plate ranged from 6 mm on the sides to 12 mm on the nose and floor, which may account for the survival of this 'bathtub' section.

No. 102/2 August 1943

Grupul 8 asalt

Technical Specifications* of the Henschel Hs 129 B-2 in Service with *Grupul 8 Asalt*

[*under operational conditions]

Engines: Gnome-Rhône 14M

Power: 700 hp at 3030 RPM and 1.50 [atm.] intake pressure, 0 m height (at takeoff),

660 hp at 2750 RPM and 1.25 [atm.] intake pressure, 4000 m height,

520 hp at 2350 RPM and 1.10 [atm.] intake pressure, 4000 m height

Speed: max. 365 km/h, in horizontal flight, no bomb load,

336 km/h, cruising speed, no bomb load, flying alone,

max. 345 km/h, with full bomb load, flying alone,

316 km/h, cruising speed, with full bomb load, flying alone,

approx. 300 km/h, cruising speed, with full bomb load, flying in formation

Climbing: 1.9 sec. to 1000 m, 3.8 sec. to 2000 m, 5.8 sec. to 3000 m, 7.9 sec. to 4000 m

Ceiling: max. 4000 m, operational height: 0-1200 m

Range: 30 min. at max. speed, 1.45 hrs. at cruising speed

Bomb load: 6 x 50 kg (300 kg). There is no other bombload combination possibility

Bomb racks: ETC 50 VIID

On-board weapons: 2 x 20 mm cal. Mauser cannon (the cannon barrel can be switched with a 15 mm Rheinmetall machine gun's barrel).

2 x 7.92 mm cal. Rheinmetall MG 17 machine guns

Gunsight: Revi C.12C, simple type

Most common faults: Breaks in the hydraulic system. Because the hydraulic lines are manufactured of poor quality rubber, they are easily eaten by the brake fluid.

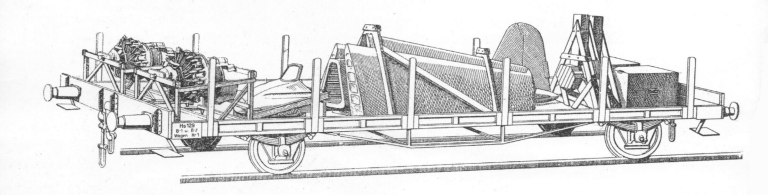

△ This drawing taken from RLM handbook D.(Luft)T.2129 B-1 u. B-2 part 10, shows how the Hs 129 could be transported by rail. All handbooks prepared by the RLM contained a section on how any aircraft could be transported by this means.